# CALLED TO LEAD

## WISDOM FOR THE NEXT GENERATION OF AFRICAN AMERICAN LEADERS

Edited by

**Eugene Seals**
and
**Matthew Parker**

A Quality Book™

# Called to Lead

## Wisdom for the Next Generation of African American Leaders

Edited by Eugene Seals and Matthew Parker

Printed in the United States of America.

Published by
Moody Press
Chicago, Illinois
and
Quality Publishing Systems
Box 339635
Farmington Hills, Michigan 48333

# DEDICATION

To Tom Skinner and all those pioneers who paved the way for the current generation of leaders.

Never give in, never give in, never, never, never, never – in nothing, great or small, large or petty – never give in except to convictions of honor and good sense.

— Winston Churchill
(Address at Harrow School
October 29, 1941)

# CONTENTS

# Preface

by Matthew Parker

*Matthew Parker, M.A., is president of The Institute for Black Family Development, a multi-faceted ministry which designs and coordinates programs designed to strengthen the Black family.*

The best leaders accomplish goals without making people feel that they have been led. In the spring of 1969, African American evangelist Tom Skinner preached in the chapel at Grand Rapids School of Bible and Music. One of the young students in the audience was this writer, who now is the president of a Christian organization. I remain impressed at how Skinner took me aside, spent time and money on me, and encouraged me to grow as a leader. He became a mentor to me from that point forward; and what he did for me, he did for others as well.

Many African American leaders now active in missions, leadership development, pastoring, publishing, and other fields owe a debt to Tom Skinner. His leadership is responsible for networking and encouraging African-American-led ministries. It was important to him to help leaders realize they are not as alone as they used to think.

This book is written by seventeen African American leaders like Skinner who share a vignette of their lives and leadership style with others. The qualities and character that they possess are expressed in their own way.

It is their desire to be helpful to you. Accordingly, they invest every effort to provide clear direction to the reader. Open and candid in what they offer, they demonstrate honesty and trust.

These leaders lift up the value of coaching and supporting people, praising them for good performance more often than criticizing them for problem performance. They point out how important it is to follow up on important issues and actions in a timely fashion. In addition, they note that selecting and developing good workers is critical to the success of the ministry.

Our authors underscore the importance of encouraging innovation while at the same time helping people to make clear-cut decisions when they need assistance. Above all – contrary to one popular misconception of leadership – our authors demonstrate high levels of integrity in the workplace, at home, in the ministry, and at church.

As you read, it is my desire that you would begin to implement the gems of this book in your own life and ministry.

Matthew Parker, President
Institute for Black Family Development

# 1

## Why This Book?

by Eugene Seals

An effective leader is one who inspires people to follow him toward a goal. It is comparatively easy to attain the related titles of owner, founder, manager, president, executive director, supervisor, and the like – by good work, by good fortune, by bribery, even by mistake. But the title of leader has to be earned. People have to see in you something that makes them believe that you can help them achieve some goal, such as fulfilling the will of God for their lives. Only when you have their trust and respect are you a leader.

Our Lord raises up leaders without regard to whether or not they have gone to the Ivy League institutions of higher learning. John Perkins, one of our authors, notes that when he came up, three years of elementary school was all that he was able to complete before he was taken out to work in the cotton fields of Mississippi. Little did anyone know at that time that God would call John to return to Mississippi to launch a small work in rural Mendenhall, that it would give rise to an international movement which today is known as the Christian Community Development Association, and that it would eventually attract observers not only from all over America, but also from as far away as New Zealand down under.

We know of others who have been called from humble backgrounds to leadership. For example, Mrs. Sarah Small of the Roxbury section of Boston had no idea when she left school before she finished the ninth grade that she would be led to march with Dr. Martin Luther King, Jr., or that she would later be called to lead the chapel ministry at the University of Massachusetts. In addition, the obvious hand of God on her work with the underprivileged through the Packard Manse ministry has led Ph.D.s, doctors of divinity, pastors, and others to seek her advice on how to operate such a ministry.

You are no doubt aware of similar leaders in your own circles. The remarkable thing about such leaders is that most did not aspire to leadership. Their parents probably never rocked their cradle singing a "lullaby of success" for them. They no doubt saw their lack of formal training as qualifying them for a more traditional existence, perhaps as a follower, perhaps impacting a handful of relatives and close friends. They may have been content, as was the prophet Amos, to humbly but diligently tend their "sheep and sycamore tree" business. It is only in retrospect that they, we, and the world can see that God had other plans for them.

There are many individuals like Dr. Perkins and Mrs. Small. Some of them are in the middle of their ministries. Others are just getting started. Still others may be wrestling with God to see who will win. The task we gave a broad assortment of experienced African American leaders was to reflect on the history of their ministries and to share with other leaders one suggestion which would assist them in doing a better job for the Lord. Some of the answers are straightforward, but powerful. Others are a bit less predictable.

For instance, *Dr. A. Charles Ware,* president of Baptist Bible College, launches the dialogue by asserting that character is one of the most important ingredients in biblical leadership. Many of us have been disappointed at the lack of character, not only in business people with whom we have dealt, but especially in Christian leaders. Ware challenges us to note the damage that such a lack does to the mission of the business or ministry. He points us to the biblical standard for leadership selection in 1 Timothy 3. Sometimes it may seem that following God's way takes too long to get things done. It may seem, further, that the rewards are not right. Someone else may get the credit for what we do. Ware cautions us not to compromise our character in trying to correct what we consider to be slow progress or incorrect rewards. After all, our character is an integral part of our mission.

*Dr. John Perkins,* publisher of *Urban Family* magazine, is an internationally recognized pioneer who challenges us to fill the leadership vacuum by doing what we can with what we have. He describes the three basic ingredients that are needed if one is to be an effective leader and shows us the difference between bossism and leadership.

You may know from personal experience the terror that comes over a leader. You wake at three o'clock in the morning in a cold sweat, wondering, "Why are we doing what we are doing?" It is not a question of whether the ministry is thriving. The organization may or may not be growing hand over fist. It may or may not be tearing down barns and building bigger ones. Hardly anything is more paramount than that the leadership come to grips with the question: "Are we doing the right thing; or are we simply doing the thing right?" The results of such an exercise are invariably beneficial.

*Attorney Roland G. Hardy, Jr.,* asks us to face that question head on by challenging us not to get in the game if we don't plan to win. As simple as that may sound, he illustrates his point profoundly as he uses the matter of warfare as an analogy to illustrate how a simple mission statement can keep a ministry from being unsuccessful (or successful at doing the wrong thing). His emphasis on planning can usually be addressed by scheduling regular meetings to deal with that dimension of leadership. It is not always easy to do what is right; but to fail to plan is to plan to fail. Making planning a prominent agenda item for your management team and your board of directors may yield surprising results.

Such planning is often done in the leader's head. He or she may *know* where the organization should go. But the problem is that other team players may be working at what they *think* the leader is thinking. The mission statement must be reduced to writing, reviewed regularly, and revised at least once every five years.

Highlighting the most essential element of any successful Christian enterprise, *Joseph C. Jeter, Sr.,* president of Have Christ Will Travel, issues a call to prayer for our ministries. He notes that prayer is not only essential and exciting, it also allows the leader to fellowship with God and to enjoy the blessing of results that often exceed our expectations.

*Dolphus Weary,* president of The Mendenhall Ministries, suggests that ministries formulate long-range plans for developing future leaders. His own experience in moving into leadership of the premier work in rural Christian community development is truly remarkable. Dolphus hopes that readers will learn from the experiences he had as he began to move into leadership.

Dolphus puts it on the table: It is intimidating to follow in the footsteps of a man like John Perkins. If you are a dynamic leader today, what can you do to reduce this kind of anxiety for your successor? Part of the planning for your ministry should address how to prepare your successor. Too many ministries retire when the founder dies, retires, or accepts a call to another location.

One of the difficult issues that leaders face is what seems to be gross immaturity and inexperience on the part of the people in the ministry. Choosing a successor from among them may look impossible. Often taking a second look at those people may reveal a diamond in the rough. While the founding leader may have been extraordinary, God does not always require that His leaders be exceptional from birth. As Barbara Walton says, leaders are made, not born. But the process is not complete even after the selection of the successor. Careful planning and implementation are required in order to pass the baton in the best way to assure that your team makes a good showing in the race.

*Dr. Delores L. Kennedy-Williams,* president of the Women's Commission, African Methodist Episcopal Church, discusses the way in which she and her colleagues have taken women's group leadership from the informal dimension of the kitchen table to the intensity and impact of the boardroom. In the process, they discovered the place of sound management principles and practices.

*Sherry Sherrod DuPree,* chairperson of the Rosewood Massacre Forum, a group of educators involved in preserving Black history, points out the invaluable contribution of a number of nineteenth and twentieth century Black women leaders. Her historical perspective highlights how women have been able to be effective in addressing social and spiritual needs in our world in spite of prevailing attitudes in the church and in the world. There is a definite trend whereby our Black young ladies are experiencing greater educational achievement than our young men. There is a corresponding difference in their abilities to function in today's church and the world. Women are more and more accepting the challenge of obtaining higher education and assuming the mantle of leadership in the church and in Christian organizations. DuPree feels that this is essential if we are not to fall further behind in the battle against Satan and against such challenges as poverty, AIDS, racism, aging, and the like.

It is becoming more and more obvious that African Americans need to own and operate more of the major institutions that impact our lives. *Dr. Melvin Banks* relates how a seed planted in his mind when he was eleven years old sprang up as Urban Ministries, Inc., a significant publisher of Sunday school literature and other materials for the African American church.

Banks reminisces that the road was not easy, that a lot of prayer and hard work were required every step of the way. One can't help but think that he might have benefited from reading this book had it been available twenty years ago. His chapter touches on his discovery of a number of the points raised by the other authors: the need to develop a clearly focused mission statement, to share the vision with others, to establish goals, to set priorities, to develop strategies, and to be persistent.

*Beverly Yates,* of Circle Y Ranch Bible Camp, recounts her own leadership development and how she embraced concepts she learned along the way. Her idea of developing new leaders is to work yourself out of a job by training a successor from your first day on the job. This recommendation would result in a more rapid deployment of sufficient numbers of Christian leaders to meet the needs of this present age.

In a similar vein, *Russell Knight,* president of Chicago Urban Reconciliation Enterprise, summarizes the history of leadership development in the African American church and community. He makes a case for more emphasis on a team approach to ministry in order to share the load and to use the gifts which the Lord gives to the body.

*Dr. Clarence Walker,* president of Clarence Walker Ministries, presents a topic that we might prefer to avoid: suffering at the hands of people – with emphasis on wounds inflicted by one man on another. Using the four types of "man wounds" as a point of departure, Walker shows how suffering is often developmental and fits into God's plans for us.

*Dr. Mary Ross,* president of the Women's Department, National Baptist Convention, U.S.A., Inc., draws attention to how Jesus held women in high regard. She describes the new possibilities for women and men as exhilarating and highlights the growing need for all sorts of ministries in the family, church, and society. Given the present crisis, it is imperative that we get rid of many of the old models of ministry and seek God's direction for addressing the problems at hand. Ross enumerates several national programs and proposes specific steps that leaders can take.

*Ja'Ola Walker,* vice-president of Clarence Walker Ministries, has observed from her years of leadership and counseling that God is calling for a new breed of leaders: men and women who have a supernatural anointing of God exploding in us and touching those around us. The mission needs to be born out of a divine burden. The leader must keep on hearing from heaven through a vital daily relation with our heavenly Father. A healthy accountability system will help keep us on track and out of the pitfalls that the enemy places before and around us. Finally, Walker reminds us that leaders recognize that their families are the most important part of their ministries.

*Lorraine Elizabeth Williams*, of the Pittsburgh Leadership Foundation, is all too aware of the dynamics of working as leader for various helpless, underprivileged people in her community. She calls for the development of more women to fill the growing demand for leaders, and she lists some essentials needed in effective leadership development.

*Barbara Walton*, in retrospect, now knows that leaders are made – not born. Allowing herself to be used in the Lord's service, she found that cooking and talking provided the opportunity for her to have an impact on the development of several of today's leaders. Her plea is that we who are older and more experienced should mentor the young people who are coming along. We have no way of knowing whether that untutored and unlearned young man or woman may be called to lead a major work in our urban centers or to become mentor to yet another generation of leaders. Faithfulness to God has a way of producing results beyond any that we dare ask or think.

*Eugene Seals,* former executive director of Detroit Rescue Mission Ministries, reviews some of the principles he pursued following being called to lead an existing organization. Rather than take the somewhat common approach of revising everything that worked for his predecessor, Seals used biblical principles to ascertain whether existing structures were workable in achieving the organization's mission and made only essential changes.

It is a truism that people are the most important part of ministry. Seals expanded the scope of people to include not only the clients of the various programs, but also the employees who did the counseling, the cooking, the cleaning, and the counting as well. People development was a priority.

Seals observes that the Christian organization has a responsibility to seek and exploit responsible uses of technology and other tools of organization. Further, management cannot be done from the ivory tower. A leader needs to earn the respect of colleagues and clients. Leadership requires a lot of walking around the organization.

The authors of this book represent a number of Christian traditions and a variety of perspectives. While all of them agree on the central doctrines of the Christian faith, there may be some difference of interpretation on various other items. Consequently, the opinions expressed belong to the author of each chapter and not necessarily to other contributors.

What is our purpose? Frankly it is our prayer that the Lord's work will move ahead better as a result of your reading this book. The Bible teaches that in the multitude of counselors, there is safety. We have assembled seventeen leaders to provide you with what each considers to be a word of wisdom which he or she wants to pass along to other leaders. Their reward will be to hear that your ministry benefited in some small way as a result of their labor of love.

# 2

---

# A Call to Leadership Is a Call to Character

by A. Charles Ware

*A. Charles Ware, D.D., of Indianapolis, Indiana, is president of Baptist Bible College.*

A call to leadership is first of all a call to character. Paul observes that the desire for leadership (bishop or deacon) is good; but character is a prerequisite for the office (1 Timothy 3). Character in leadership is a matter of integrity before God, before yourself, before your family, before your team, and before your publics.

Leadership in the Kingdom of God requires character that is becoming of children of the King. Today the Kingdom message is being communicated with tantalizing effects upon the senses to the masses through high-tech media. Some ministries have become major productions requiring a large supporting cast. The superstar must have a charming personality, attractive appearance, and be a charismatic communicator. Although it is acknowledged that God can and does raise up large ministries, the fall of many "successful" leaders over the past two decades should raise some serious questions about our formula for leadership. The exposure of lying, deception, pride, sexual immorality, and lack of accountability should make it clear that character has become an all-too-often forgotten ingredient in leadership. It is easier to "create a good public image" than to become recreated in the image of Christ. A godly leader recognizes that the work belongs to God. We have been privileged not only to be saved by grace, but also to participate in the advancement of the Kingdom of God. We are stewards, not owners. Therefore, we should trust God for the prosperity of the ministry and not depend on personal promotion. Internal corruption makes one susceptible to controlling influences other than God. Such corruption may result in an attractive ministry led by an ungodly man or woman. A holy heart is an asset when one seeks the help of God's hand in ministry. A wise man said, "Above all else, guard your heart, for it is the wellspring of life" (Proverbs 4:23).

Leadership in the Kingdom is a partnership. It is wise to understand which responsibilities are God's and which are ours. We cannot perform God's responsibilities and He will not perform ours. God's program is larger than any one person. An honest evaluation of our God-given strengths and weaknesses is a profitable exercise. Too many leaders have a tendency to overestimate their own importance (Romans 12:3). However, human limitations demand that we focus on our duties, develop new leaders, and delegate responsibilities (Exodus 18; Acts 6:1-7). The desire to control and receive the credit can cause people to be perceived as mere ends to personal gain. We should rejoice at the privilege that God has given us to participate in the success of others whom He is also using in the advancement of His Kingdom. How often is the development of leaders delayed or Kingdom issues overlooked because jealousy, envy, pride, bitterness, and so forth rule in the heart of a leader! One of our greatest joys should be the success of those with whom we serve. Good leadership places priority on developing others. Their success results in the advancement of the Kingdom. Even in the secular realm, sales managers acknowledge that they make their quotas only when their sales people make their quotas.

As stewards, Kingdom leaders must acknowledge God's sovereign control, follow God's commands, and rest in God's love. In a culture of competition, where numbers and ratings often become the criteria for promotion and prosperity, it is easy to forget that promotion in the Kingdom comes from the Lord, the real owner of our gifts, talents, and ministries. Seeking to build a ministry, one may be seduced by polls, surveys, and expert opinion to invest one's life in works which, although praised by men, may well be rejected by God (1 Corinthians 3:11-22).

Too many are sacrificing their families on the altar of ministry. Marriage is not a qualification for ministry, but a married leader must have a solid marriage and family situation (1 Timothy 3:2-5). The Kingdom requires that married leaders' priorities are to be different than the priorities of singles (1 Corinthians 7:32-35). A Kingdom leader must consciously and continually acknowledge that the work is the Lord's and he or she is but a servant. One's service is not only to the ministry, but to one's family as well.

God is still raising up leaders who will do what is in His heart and mind. Kingdom leaders are not driven by the market but by the divine manual, the Bible. We should be more concerned about being prophetically (biblically) correct than politically correct. In both leadership and ministry, our policies and procedures should manifest proper biblical interpretation and application. Therefore, the issue is not simply whether something is legal but rather is it just and right before God. The issue in public relations is not whether it looks and sounds good, but whether it is true and necessary to communicate. The issue in relevance is not only what my history, culture, tradition, peers, and so forth dictate, but what divine revelation demands. Impartial, biblical, godly, prophetic leadership is a difficult task. For example, the flirtation between civil rights and immorality (especially homosexuality) demands discernment and clear statements of truth. The bondage of conscience by "Blackness" requires boldness to stand by biblical standards of righteousness. The Scriptures give clear advice to leaders who desire to save both themselves and those who hear them (1 Timothy 4:15-16):

1. Meditate on scriptural principles;
2. Activate scriptural principles in life; and
3. Evaluate your doctrine and life in the light of scriptural principles.

Contrary to popular opinion, the Bible teaches that one's private life (especially in the moral arena) not only affects the person but also qualifies or disqualifies him or her for public ministry (1 Timothy 3). Kingdom leadership requires rising above arrogance, anger, and fear of man to mediate the will of God without partiality. Our various publics deserve such leadership from those representing the King.

## Victor, not Victim

One must seek the grace of God in order to be a victor rather than a victim of the challenges of life. Integrity demands that one faithfully give his or her very best to every opportunity God sovereignly brings before him or her. It is easy for African Americans to adopt a victim mentality. Some are immobilized by the notion that there is no need to study, work, or dream because the "White man" will not allow them to succeed.

When I was in seminary (with a majority White enrollment) the dean confided that he did not know of one Bible college that would seriously consider hiring a Black professor. It is amusing to me that today I am not only a professor but also the president of a Bible college! God is in control. Prayer, holy living, and perseverance are honored by God. Christian leaders must learn to labor, not for what they can see, but rather for Whom they see.

The scars of racism have caused many to get sidetracked and even to give up. We need a generation of Josephs who understand that even if man meant it for evil, God meant it for good. The question is: When the King calls upon us to lead in His Kingdom, will we be ready spiritually, physically, and mentally? The following disciplines will help one to be ready for leadership:

1. Seize opportunities afforded you instead of complaining about lack of opportunities.

2. Work hard at every assignment. Avoid making excuses for laziness.

3. Exercise forgiveness. Become a channel of God's reconciling grace.

4. Commit yourself to character development and personal growth.

5. Trust God.

6. Persevere in righteousness, realizing that the judge of all the earth will do right.

## Radical Obedience

A Kingdom leader's character is manifested in obedience to the Word of God (James 1:18-25). God's work must be performed according to the principles contained in His Word. Therefore, Kingdom leaders need to gain a clear understanding of the Word so their work may be approved by Him (2 Timothy 2:15).

The question is not whether the culture and/or corporation will accept lying, stealing, false accusations, sexual immorality, and so forth; but what does the Word of God say? Something may be legally right but biblically wrong. Something may be legally wrong but biblically right! Kingdom leaders must be committed to the Scriptures. Such commitment may be enhanced by the following disciplines:

1. Read the Scriptures daily (Proverbs has many leadership principles).

2. Study the Scriptures regularly.

3. Apply the principles discerned to leadership.

4. Practice obeying the Scriptures, especially those relating to inward character.

5. Pray according to the Scriptures.

Kingdom leaders must rest in the love of the King. Biblical leadership can be lonely. Biblical integrity and obedience are not popular, even among some in the Christian community today. For many, culture has become more important than Christ. A "Black thing" has become more important than a biblical thing. Vindictive statements and actions have become greater motivators than forgiveness and love. Our service, ultimately, is not to culture, tradition, or denomination, but to God who is the searcher of the heart. God does not deny the past or excuse the present sins of saints and sinners. Rather, He forgives and frees all from our sins if we ask. Kingdom leaders must learn that our ultimate approval will be in the fact that God is pleased with our character and leadership. Again, faithfulness is required of stewards, even in the face of insurmountable odds (1 Corinthians 4:1-5).

## The Value of Security and Contentment

Personal security and contentment frees a leader to be more concerned about the people to whom he ministers than about himself (Philippians 4:10-19). Leadership faces the danger of being perverted by personal insecurity agendas which are contrary to Kingdom values. Kingdom leaders must have good memories. Remember:

1. Your salvation.

2. Your communion with the living God.

3. Your privilege to serve in the Kingdom program.

4. The judgment, when all our actions and attitudes will be rewarded.

Character in leadership is crucial. The Bible says, "Righteousness exalts a nation, but sin is a disgrace to any people" (Proverbs 14:34). Society may ignore it, but the sovereign Savior demands character in Kingdom leaders. The true quality of one's leadership will not be judged by an opinion poll, but by omnipotent examination. As Kingdom leaders, we should be guided by the King's agenda, values, and love.

As a servant of the Supreme Controller of all things, the Kingdom leader should commit the ultimate "success" of the ministry to God. While we may obtain some profitable ideas from Madison Avenue and corporate America, the Christian leader must never forget that man is not the master of his own fate. In a climate where competency, competitiveness, and charisma are praised while character is overlooked, Christian leaders must beware. Good planning and diligent management are commended by God, but it is arrogance to believe that the success or failure of God's ministry rests entirely upon human ingenuity and strength.

Furthermore, it is an attack upon both the wisdom and the power of God to believe that His work is best served by deceit and disobedience. I have found it profitable to remind myself periodically that the work of God began before I was born, and that the work will continue after my death. This truth frees me from the bondage of trying to promote the ministry by human wisdom and energy alone. It also creates in me a holy reverence, realizing that God can and will replace an unholy servant.

Finally, Kingdom leaders must not prostitute their calling for popularity, promotion, prosperity, pleasure, or peer approval. We must acknowledge that God has sovereignly placed us in leadership to communicate His message and carry out His work according to His command. A call to leadership is a call to character.

# 3

## Filling the Leadership Vacuum

by John M. Perkins

*John M. Perkins, Litt.D., of Pasadena, California, is the publisher of* Urban Family *magazine. Founder and chair of the Christian Community Development Association, he has authored numerous books, including* Beyond Charity *and* He's My Brother.

"I did what I could with what I had." Supreme Court Justice Thurgood Marshall's words describe me to a T. Always trying to understand the times in which we live, I continue to this day to strive to give the best leadership I can.

It is extremely important for leaders to understand the times in which they live and to work for justice in the best way they know during their lifetime. I believe that I have lived at a crucial time in history. And I believe that God used the circumstances of my young life to prepare me for leadership.

I was born in Mississippi in 1930. My mother died when I was seven months old; and my father gave the five of us children to his mother, Grandma Babe, who had mothered nineteen children of her own. We lived under the southern plantation system, designed to keep Blacks in subjugation. This system remained until the Civil Rights Act of 1965.

It was a very serious time for Blacks in this country. In his book, *Mississippi: The Closed Society*, Dr.

James Silver suggests that everything in the Black man's environment was designed to make him feel inferior – to make him feel like a "nigger." He was to be a Sambo or a Stepin Fetchit.[1] A Black man was expected to be happy while he and his loved ones lived in poverty and misery. Never, never was he to use his skills to cast off the oppression in his life.

I can remember many incidents of brutality and hostility in the little town of New Hebron where I lived. These were designed to keep us in "our place." I remember when a young Black man named J. C. Smith returned home after spending some years in the military service during World War II. Having attained the rank of sergeant, he was proud to have served his country. But many of the White folks saw him as being uppity and arrogant. To remind him of his "place," one day a group of Whites beat him nearly to death right on the main street of the town. This was the atmosphere in which I grew up.

I come from a family of bootleggers and gamblers; so I learned early about risk, about managing fear, and about economic opportunity. I still remember the day that I learned that the problems of the Black community were more than social – that they were also economic. I recall working for a White man all day, expecting to get $1.50. When the day ended he gave me only 15 cents. I felt dehumanized and exploited, realizing that I was little more than a slave. But I learned a valuable lesson. This man owned the resources; so he made the rules. And if I was going to make it in this society, I too would have to obtain

---

[1]In order to work in the movies, Stepin Fetchit, a popular African American comedian, was forced to accept only roles where he played the buffoon, a grossly exaggerated, demeaning, shuffling, false stereotype of the Black man.

the mules, wagon, hay, and field that were the essence of production at that time.

This was also a crucial time for Blacks in another way. White women, especially those in the North, began entering the workforce in unprecedented numbers. Many Black women began heading north to take advantage of the jobs being offered in these women's homes. Many families were broken within the Black community because their husbands often remained behind. At the same time, many Black men were migrating North looking for job opportunities and leaving their families behind.

When I was sixteen years old, my own brother was killed in a racial incident while in line at a movie theater in New Hebron. Fed up with the oppression, I – like so many other young Blacks – left Mississippi with no intention of ever returning to live. I moved to California and got a job. When the Korean War erupted, I went into the Service and got married to Vera Mae. I spent my tour of duty on Okinawa. After my military time, I returned home to California and began working for a large food chain. I was content just being a husband and father who could provide a decent living for my family.

The next significant event in my life was when my oldest son Spencer began to attend Sunday school and Good News Club at the age of four. The positive effect this had on his young life eventually led me to give my life to God in 1957. After my conversion, the Lord led me to return to Mississippi in 1960. For the next eight years or so, I taught the Gospel to young children in public schools all across central Mississippi and began a youth ministry and church in the small town of Mendenhall, just south of the capital city of Jackson.

The civil rights movement of the 1960s helped me to see clearly the need for holistic development in our little town. It became ever so plain how the system was set up to keep the Black community oppressed. I also realized that we were continually losing our best resources – the one thing that could give us hope for the future – our young people. Because they saw and felt the social and economic oppression, they were leaving for the North as soon as they graduated from high school. In order for this to change, the system had to be confronted.

It was this intense desire to throw off the oppression of our community, combined with my biblical understanding of God's concern for justice, that thrust me into leadership. But, of course, leadership was not without its risks. When I led a protest march against the wrongful jailing of a young man who had supposedly phoned a White woman and asked her for a date, I began to understand that leaders must have the courage of their conviction even if it means facing the threat of death. The protest escalated into a two-month demonstration against the powers of our little town and finally resulted in my being beaten almost to the point of death at the hands of White police, the sheriff, and the highway patrol in the nearby town of Brandon.

But I am convinced that through all of this, God was preparing me for a specific type of leadership. God had given me a passion for justice that will forever be imprinted upon my soul. He also showed me that justice must go hand in hand with reconciliation. The aches, the pains, and the scars on my body are a constant reminder lest I forget my mission. What was meant for evil, God used for good. And for the past twenty-five years my leadership has had a specific purpose – justice and reconciliation.

Following are a number of important elements that I have found to be helpful over the years.

## Basic Leadership

President Eisenhower summed it up best. He said that a leader gets what he wants done, when he wants it done; and the people do it because they want to. In my view, there are three basic ingredients that are needed if one is to be an effective leader.

1. An understanding of how energy works.
2. A knowledge of his environment.
3. A faith that sustains him in spite of the threat of economic and physical hardship.

First, it is important that the leader understands how energy flows. He should know when and how to release it. It is vital that the leader receive from the ministry a certain joy and fulfillment which not only energizes him, but also motivates those around him.

Next, the leader must have a deep love for the people he is leading. He should be knowledgeable about the environment in which the people live. Otherwise he puts them at unnecessary risk that he may not be willing to take himself. The very fact that I lived in Mississippi as a young man and understood the system gave me insight into how to go about challenging it.

Third, it is crucial that while the leader is providing leadership in a difficult situation, that he have creative faith in God, confidence in himself, a willingness to make sacrifices in relationship to the goals that he has set, and a belief that the task will be achieved even if it costs him his own life.

Creative leadership creates resources. The real leader does not have to exploit his people or manipulate the public to obtain resources. Paul always seemed to have adequate resources from the people around him. Lydia and others did not stand by and see Paul begging in order to pay his bills while he ministered to the people. The leader should have the confidence to go forward, never worrying about his own survival.

Fannie Lou Hamer, the main indigenous leader when the Civil Rights movement entered Mississippi, was willing to give up her position of limited privilege on the plantation and give energetic leadership in confronting injustice in the Mississippi Delta. She was able to lead effectively because the people were wise enough to provide the necessary resources for her family when the inevitable economic attack came. In the same way, I have been blessed to have a reasonable amount of that same type of security throughout my ministry. This support from friends who believed in what we were doing enabled me to stand firm at a time when I knew our stand would cost us the loss of financial support from many Whites.

### Effective Leadership

One model of an effective leader can be seen in the book of Esther. Mordecai raised the orphaned Esther as his own daughter after the death of her mother and father. From the time she was young, he instilled certain qualities in her:

*1. Know yourself.*

Be what you are. Avoid trying to appear being what you are not. Develop your strengths. Find others to compensate for your weaknesses.

*2. Communicate clearly and precisely.*

Take advantage of every opportunity. Most people do not want to be "told" what to do. A real leader gets people together and goes over a game plan making sure everyone knows what part he plays.

### 3. *Make decisions.*

The faster you make a decision the more effectiveness you will have as a leader. Do not make decisions in a vacuum. You need a keen sense of when to act.

### 4. *Have well-defined goals.*

Do what is necessary to see that the goals are reached.

### 5. *Strive to develop people's self-confidence to a level of performance beyond their expectations.*

Leaders enrich others and are known by the personalities they enrich as they allow others to achieve aims and goals that they have for themselves.

## Bosses vs. Leaders

The January/February 1995 edition of Promise Keepers' *New Man* magazine (Strang Communications, used by permission) notes a few key differences between those who boss and those who lead:

A *Boss* creates fear.
A *Leader* creates excitement.

*Bossism* creates resentment.
*Leadership* breeds enthusiasm.

A *Boss* says "I."
A *Leader* says "We."

A *Boss* fixes blame.
A *Leader* fixes mistakes.

A *Boss* knows how.
A *Leader* shows how.

*Bossism* makes work drudgery.
*Leadership* makes work interesting.

A *Boss* relies on authority.
A *Leader* relies on cooperation.

A *Boss* drives.
A *Leader* leads.

One who intends to give spiritual leadership must have a holistic understanding of the Gospel. He or she must see the Body of Christ as the people of God living and working for a common cause in relationship together. He or she must teach by example, organizing people to live out their common vision within a geographical neighborhood. Today's leaders need to be involved in moving the people of a particular area toward the goals which they have established for themselves. I have found a wealth of wisdom in an old Chinese proverb and have patterned much of my grass-roots leadership style from it:

Go to the people;
Live among them.
Love them.
Learn from them.
Plan with them.
Start with what they know.
Build on what they have.

And when the best leaders leave,
The people will say,
"We did it ourselves."

Finally, a person in leadership must be ever learning. In addition to the normal skills and gifts, here are a number of characteristics which are of the utmost importance.

### 1. A leader must learn how to stand alone.

Spending time with God will enable a leader's character to be developed. As a visionary you will have times when you will stand alone. You must have the courage to follow through on your convictions. Gaining strength from being alone with God will give you the stamina needed.

## 2. *A leader must know how to plan.*

Set goals, and then manage time effectively. Organize energy around a plan. Work the plan.

## 3. *A leader must know how to live with pain.*

A leader must be able to see times of pain, especially the pain of criticism, as an opportunity to sharpen his vision. Do not discount criticism too quickly.

In urban America we face a crisis: a lack of genuine leadership. Today's leaders are not willing to suffer the pain that builds character. Therefore, instead of giving strong leadership, many waver back and forth like a tree in gusting crosswinds. My prayer is that the next generation will give birth to leaders who understand and appreciate their heritage, and who have a deep concern and burden to lead our people to a higher level of excellence even when it is not popular or comfortable. The future of our cities depends on it.

# 4

# Strategic Planning: Don't Get in the War if You Don't Plan to Win

by Roland G. Hardy, Jr.

*Roland G. Hardy, Jr., J.D., is president of Renaissance Productions, publisher of* Beyond Roots: In Search of Blacks in the Bible. *An attorney, he serves as counsel to churches and ministries throughout the nation. Hardy is also former senior vice president of The Urban Alternative.*

In 1963, the United States sent its first military troops into Vietnam. A decision had been made to enter the war. As our troops began to occupy South Vietnamese villages, it became immediately clear that the United States had forgotten something. Our military leadership had failed to specify our mission. Was the mission to oversee a conflict between relatives, to serve as a peacekeeping agent, to provide non-combat military advice to the South Vietnamese, or what?

In addition to being saddled with an unclear mission, U.S. troops were ill-prepared for the fight. They knew very little about several critical items: Vietnamese culture and customs, the art of jungle warfare, and the enemy's military tactics. The outcome was predictable. After twelve years of fighting, a sobering

50,000-plus fatalities, and untold injuries, the United States withdrew its troops without measurable success. Why did the U.S. involvement end in defeat? Because the United States had forgotten the most basic element of warfare: a comprehensive strategic plan for winning. Similarly, many churches and ministries fail to accomplish their mission because they do not engage in comprehensive strategic planning.

## Why Strategic Planning?

Although definitions vary from planner to planner, there is some consensus among authors and managers regarding the essential elements involved in strategic planning: a purpose, objectives, external and internal assessments, a long-term strategy, realistic action plans, and regular evaluations. For the purpose of this chapter, I will define strategic planning as the process of:

1. Identifying your purpose and objectives;

2. Assessing the community around you as well as your internal strengths and weaknesses;

3. Establishing realistic action plans; and

4. Evaluating your performance in achieving your purpose and objectives.

Strategic planning begins with determining who should be involved in the planning process. In the African American church, planning participants tend to be limited to the pastor and the deacon, executive, or elder boards. This approach limits input into the planning process and causes the planning to be superficial and visionary as compared to being detailed and realistic.

In the local church, the planning team should include the following:

1. The pastor;
2. The deacon, elder, trustee, steward, and executive boards;
3. The associate and assistant ministers; and
4. Ministry leaders.

In the Christian organization, the board of directors, officers, and key management personnel should participate in the strategic planning.

## The Mission Statement

Once the strategic planning team has been assembled, its initial task is to identify and document the organization's mission. This is accomplished in the form of a mission statement which defines the nature of the organization and its reason for existence. (See Examples 1 and 2.)

### *Example 1*

<u>Mt. Zion Baptist Church Mission Statement</u>

Mt. Zion Baptist Church has been organized to:
- promote the Gospel of Jesus Christ through public worship, personal and corporate evangelism, and missionary outreach;
- teach and train its members in the observance of biblical Christianity; and
- conduct other activities designed to advance the Kingdom of God through Jesus Christ.

*Example 2*

---

## The Year of the Family Ministry Mission Statement

To mount a campaign designed to counteract the prevailing anti-Christian perspective of the family and to serve as a catalyst for the re-introduction of biblical family standards within the urban community.

---

The mission statement establishes a common understanding of the extent and limits of the ministry and provides clear direction for its members, staff, and participants in the performance of their duties.

### Why This Is Important

The Pentagon waged war in Southeast Asia for more than a decade, losing more than 50,000 troops. The lack of clarity of the mission may have been somewhat responsible for the confusion among the men. With the uncertainty whether they were to function as military advisers or as combat soldiers, it is somewhat understandable that the result was an unsuccessful mission and unnecessary casualties.

Unfortunately, this lack of focus is also common in Christian ministries. Church and ministry mission statements, when and if they exist, are generally so broad and vague that they fail to provide a clear definition of what the ministry is and what it should be doing. The organization finds itself unfocused and dabbling in everything from feeding the homeless to youth gang counseling. Its activities are dictated by what someone on the outside thinks it should be doing (the community, civic leaders, the government) rather than by its own mission statement. The result is that, at best, few key objectives are accomplished;

and members and staff find themselves going around in circles until they just drop out.

To be effective in implementing its God-given vision, the church or ministry must begin by distilling its vision of its purpose into a concise mission statement. Although this is a difficult process at first, its value is priceless; and it gets easier each time the organization repeats the exercise.

## Objectives

After completing the mission statement, the planning team is ready to establish objectives – the measurable accomplishments that lead to the fulfillment of the mission. These must be realistic and attainable.

Example 3 illustrates a possible starter set of objectives for our hypothetical Mt. Zion Baptist Church. Example 4 represents the actual objectives established by the planning team for the Year of the Family Ministry.

*Example 3*

---

### Mt. Zion Baptist Church
### Objectives

- To communicate the Gospel message of Jesus Christ to every household in Greenville.
- To move church members to a state of spiritual maturity within a five-year period.
- To increase the number of male members by 250 within three years.
- To build a multi-purpose facility to serve as a gym and activity center within ten years.

---

*Example 4*

---

### The Year of the Family
### Ministry Objectives

- To develop a national prayer network to support African American and Hispanic families.
- To raise a positive, yet distinctly Christian, voice through the media, concerning the urban family.
- To mobilize and give greater exposure to Christian-based ministries committed to urban families.
- To promote and explore available resources to enhance urban families.
- To equip and empower the local church in its ongoing ministry to families.
- To empower urban families.

---

## External and Internal Assessments

In order to determine the how-to's in accomplishing its objectives, the church or ministry must next assess what is going on around it as well as what is going on inside. While Mt. Zion Baptist Church can learn from strategies and tactics that have worked very well for other churches, the leadership team must keep in mind that what worked for another church may be totally inappropriate for Mt. Zion for a variety of reasons too numerous to mention here.

A large number of well-intentioned church projects have failed as a result of the local leadership not undertaking external and internal assessments with respect to their stated mission and objectives. The questions in Example 5 might be addressed profitably

by Mt. Zion Baptist Church in order to properly
assess the viability of its work as well as its strengths
and weaknesses.

*Example 5*

## External and Internal Assessment

- How many households are there in
  Greenville, and what is the access to them?
- How many households are headed by
  single females?
- How many households include teenage
  mothers?
- What is the community's socioeconomic
  profile?
- Is the community receptive to receiving the
  Gospel through a door-to-door campaign,
  media campaign, outdoor evangelistic
  meetings, etc.?
- What is the church's image in the commu-
  nity?
- What is the age and gender composition of
  the church's membership?
- How many members attend church regularly?
- How many mature Christians attend the
  church?
- Does the church have the trained
  personnel to accomplish its objectives?
- What is the church's financial position?
- What are the other churches or ministries
  in the area that service the same popula-
  tion?

Suppose the Mt. Zion Baptist Church scheduled an evangelistic door-to-door campaign for Greenville in the evenings for the first six weeks of summer. The church assembles an evangelistic team and begins training it. The team consists of four women and two men. They choose to use Bible tracts that show a White mother and father teaching their children the Scriptures around the kitchen table. The team shows up at the church at 6:30 p.m. on the first night of the campaign. They pair up and begin going to the homes in the city. After two weeks of the campaign, the team has been able to share their message with five people. Most of the homes refused to answer the door. Those who did answer said they were not interested. The five people who were cordial enough to listen to the presentation were distracted frequently by children.

*Question*: What objective was the campaign designed to meet? *Answer*: Communication of the Gospel of Jesus Christ to every household in Greenville.

An assessment of the campaign would lead us to the obvious conclusion that it was not successful in accomplishing the objective. Why? Greenville is a city of 100,000 – 70 percent of whom are African American, 28 percent Caucasian, and 2 percent Asian American. Forty percent of the 100,000 people are under the age of 25. Ninety percent of the households have income of less than $20,000 per year. Seventy percent of the families were started by unmarried teenage females. The crime rate is so high that the people don't answer their doors after dark. Most of the homes have chains or bars across the windows and doors. Further, there are three hundred Christian churches in Greenville and 20 percent of the population attend church on a regular basis. Every summer at least one church conducts a door-to-door evangelistic campaign handing out Bible tracts. The church has a reputation of being irrelevant, outdated, and hypocritical.

The door-to-door campaign did not accomplish the church's objective because the church did not consider what was going on in the community in its planning. Had it done so, it would have concluded that a door-to-door campaign would be ineffective, that its evangelistic team was too small, and that its materials did not relate to most of the people.

The planning team should have chosen a plan of action that recognized the impact of crime on the access to community homes, understood the skepticism of the community toward the church, incorporated a Gospel presentation relevant to the large percentage of unwed, teenage mothers and youth, and facilitated partnering among the various churches and ministries to maximize resources. If this planning approach had been taken, the likelihood of Mt. Zion's accomplishing its objective would have been much greater.

## Action Plan

The strategy will dictate what the organization's action plan will look like. The *action plan* takes each objective and gives it a life cycle from beginning point to achievement. This life cycle is commonly expressed in terms of goals, action points, and timetables.

For each objective, there should be a set of goals, action points, and a timetable. Each action point has a series of steps with corresponding timetables which serve as building blocks toward the accomplishment of the goals. The goals build toward the accomplishment of the objectives. Accomplishing the objectives leads to the achievement of the organization's mission.

*Example 6*

---

## Mt. Zion Baptist Church Action Plan

**Objective**: To move church members to a state of spiritual maturity within five years.

**Goal**: To assess the spiritual maturity level of all members by (specify date).

**Action Point (1)**: Establish standards for measuring spiritual maturity by (specify date).
Responsible person: pastor.

**Action Point (2)**: Establish evaluation process by (specify date).
Responsible persons: pastor and board.

**Action Point (3)**: Prepare necessary tools for evaluation by (specify date).
Responsible person: Delegated by pastor.

**Action Point (4)**: Conduct evaluation of members by (specify date).
Responsible person: pastor and board.

**Goal**: To begin spiritual growth process by (specify date).

**Action Point (1)**: Establishment of spiritual growth process by pastor and deacon board by (specify date).

**Action Point (2)**: Training of leaders by pastor to begin by (specify date).

**Action Point (3)**: Completion of initial leadership training by (specify date).

**Action Point (4)**: Assignment of families to leaders by (specify date).

## Evaluation

The last phase of strategic planning involves an evaluation to determine if the objectives have been met. Evaluation should be built into the process from the outset and conducted at predetermined intervals, such as quarterly or semi-annually. During this phase, the organization performs an assessment of its personnel, resources, objectives, and strategies. The evaluation must include appropriate rewards for accomplishments, encouragement, and – where necessary – adjustments.

## Conclusion

The goal of maximum stewardship demands that churches and ministries properly plan the most effective use of their opportunities and resources. Satan continues to roam the streets of our communities seeking those whom he may devour. The war is on for our culture. If you don't *plan* to win, don't get in the war.

# 5

---

# Prayer in Leadership

### by Joseph C. Jeter, Sr.

*Joseph C. Jeter, Sr., is founder and president of Have Christ Will Travel Ministries, a faith mission with works in the U.S.A., India, Haiti, Nova Scotia, Liberia, and Nigeria. Jeter is the author of several tracts, manuals, and books, including* Montrose Waite: Black Missionary Superb, *and* The Father of Black Faith Missions.

Without prayer, the Christian leader is helpless, whether he or she be a missionary, pastor, preacher, teacher, or auxiliary leader. The leader must understand that the program, the project, and the people are the Lord's. The leader has no power to do what needs to be done. Jesus said that all power was given to Him. A leader must stay in constant touch with the Lord who alone knows the way and has the power to cause it to occur.

## Prayer Is Essential

God is a spirit. We must worship Him in spirit and in truth. Prayer allows us to approach the throne of grace to obtain guidance from God so that His purpose may be accomplished in and through us. Through prayer, we learn the mind of Christ so that we can fall in line with His will for our lives and ministries.

Prayer anchors me to the Master and to His purpose, whether it be establishing and maintaining a work in Africa, building a church in America, teaching a Bible club in India, or caring for my family's needs. A leader must know His Master's will without a doubt, or his efforts will be empowered only by his own ability and charisma. This works very well for some people some of the time. But more than one ministry has come to a crisis of funds, spirituality, or impact because of prayerlessness on the part of the leader, the board, or the supporters.

The work is often tough. Let me dispel any illusions that it is all fun and games to be on the road and in the air 150 days out of the year – much of the time with my wife, a lot of the time without her. Over the past thirty-something years, I have ridden on roads with potholes so deep it made you wonder how any transport vehicle could make it through even one way, let alone come back to get you two weeks later. Some of the transports were so old and sagging it is truly amazing they could take large numbers of people where they needed to go. I have spent many a scorching day broken down by the side of a remote road in interior Africa, Haiti, or India waiting until another truck would come by and provide some assistance. Although the local people are accustomed to such interruptions in their schedules, we Americans sometimes find ourselves praying in such circumstances that the Lord will grant us patience and that He will do it quickly.

## Prayer Is Exciting

It is exciting to enter into prayer, spending time in worship, adoration, and fellowship, as well as receiving direction. Prayer is exciting because of the personal interaction between God and you. He alone is the source of boldness, endurance, strength, and faith.

God answered our prayers on a personal level when it was time to send my children back to school one September. Three of them had been accepted in a Christian school, but my youngest boy had not been accepted by enrollment date. My wife and I got the hurting news when we returned from a trip to Nova Scotia. We prayed and felt God telling us to take him to school. I took him to his second grade classroom, sat him down, and left. The school never called to question this action. To us, that was exciting. Today he is a vibrant Christian layman with a Ph.D.

Prayer will expand your vision as a leader. Many times, the Lord will take you to a difficult place and provoke you to pray for something more. Sometimes you must be persistent in prayer before God will reveal the answer to you. Many facets of our ministry were started under those circumstances.

God has worked in miraculous ways to sustain and empower Have Christ Will Travel Ministries (HCWT) as we minister to people in various countries. As a result of prayer, I have seen God move the hearts of Christians in America to provide beans for hungry children at our school in LaBrande, Haiti. He has supplied medicines for our clinic in Port-au-Prince. Land and a ministry center were provided in Yarmouth, Nova Scotia. Space will not permit me to list all the exciting ways I have seen God work over the last thirty years, sometimes only after we had reached the end of our rope.

Prayer for personal needs is exciting, too. In 1968, shortly after we started HCWT, I had some concern about an upcoming trip because our family vehicle had begun to fail regularly. I did not want to leave my wife and six children without reliable transportation in the City of Brotherly Love. So Catherine, the children, and I entered into a season of prayer for that need, without which the mission could not function as God intended. We had a very small amount of money and our old vehicle to put down on more reliable transportation. An ad for a used Dodge station wagon caught my eye. Catherine had prayed for a wagon to accommodate our large family. The price was $2,550. I explained to the Jewish salesman my work and why I needed a reliable vehicle.

The next morning, after the salesman had checked my credit, he told me to come over and pick out any *new* station wagon I wanted. Whereas some readers may purchase a new car every other year without giving it much thought, this was an occasion for family excitement over God's victory on our behalf. Knowing our limitations, we had prayed for a used wagon. God in His own providence provided an opportunity for the children and us to experience the meaning of the Scripture that says that God is able to give us exceedingly abundantly more than we can ask or think.

### Prayer Is Expression

The leader may not be able to express himself with people because they may not understand him or because they may try to distract or discourage him. However, a leader can always express himself to God in prayer. In Acts 16:25, Paul and Silas prayed and sang to the Lord late into the night while confined unjustly in the Philippian jail. The Lord heard them and chose to respond in a dramatic way. Without warning, there was a great earthquake which shook the very foundation of the prison, opening the doors to all the cells. In response to your hurt, desperation, and joy, God may express Himself in power, comfort, deliverance, or strength for the journey.

### Prayer Is Access

A leader must be concerned about the logistics of the ministry. He needs wisdom to know what needs to be done, when to do it, and how to do it. A leader also needs access to help in times of distress. Prayer is a great way to stay in the will of God. Jonah prayed and gained access to God. God answered Jonah. Because of His omnipotence, God always has access to us. It is by grace and the blood of our Lord Jesus that we have access to God.

The ministry of the Word of God, the power and person of the Holy Spirit, and the substitutionary atonement of our Lord and Savior give the leader the opportunity of access to the Father for encouragement in a time of trouble.

## Prayer Is Expectation

The leader must be careful to pray in faith. He must be willing to ask, to wait, and to receive with thankfulness. The answer may not always be what he desires. Remember Jonah. God may send the leader in a direction opposite to where he wants to go. The leader may be tempted to rebel. He may experience suffering, fear, and loss of valuables, necessities, and even personal security. But the leader must be assured of one thing. The victory is the Lord's. The outcome of the general situation of the leader in the will of God will be complete victory. (See Philippians 1:6, 2:13.)

God is working His sovereign will out through the leader. When the leader humbles himself to ask for power, direction, and wisdom, they will be granted. Sometimes the answer comes after lengthy trials and suffering. Moses had to confront Pharaoh ten times. Sometimes it comes quickly as when Jonah preached at Nineveh. In all cases, the timetable is the Lord's.

We can expect an answer from the same God who kept His word in sending Christ to earth through forty-two generations of Abraham's family (Matthew 1:1-17) to be born of a virgin, to live, die, rise again, and ascend into heaven from where He will return to claim those who are His own.

## Prayer Is Results

In early 1995, our mission launched a project to raise $55,000 to buy a farm to use as a ministry center in Nova Scotia. A Christian lady in Washington, D.C., asked if I really thought God would give our mission that much money. My confident response was that God had proven Himself faithful by giving $60,000 for a project nine years earlier. Because of my experience with God, the question did not offend me.

The common misconception is that God must answer Yes, or our prayer has not been answered. In my experience, God reserves the right to say No and Wait as answers also.

Further, I have learned that, as a result of prayer, a leader will experience greater results than those prayed for. A tested leader will be more effective. He will be enabled to recognize camouflage, pitfalls, and land mines on the battlefield and find a way to avoid them. He will become strong enough to make hard decisions and stand by them in the heat of battle. He will become trusted as one who knows what God wants the ministry to do in the conflict of life. His flock will trust him for the long- and short-haul of the ministry.

Further, a praying leader will become a role model for young leaders, an example to the body of Christ. A humble spirit will be reflected in the leader's manner when he is sensitive to the voice of Christ. Whatever the job entrusted to him, God will enable him to complete it. Moses, Paul, and Jesus were praying leaders. Each completed his job. A leader who prays, walks, and talks with the Master will obtain His desired results.

# 6

---

# Second Generation Leadership Development

by Dolphus Weary

*Dolphus Weary, M.A., is president of The Mendenhall Ministries. He and his team provide major, multi-faceted, holistic, church-based ministries to people in rural Mississippi, including an elementary school, a modern health clinic, a community law office, a farm, and a thrift store, to mention a few. Dolphus is the author of* I Ain't Goin' Back.

Joshua 1:6-9 introduces us to a pivotal point in the ministry of Joshua. The people of Israel were about to enter the Promised Land. Although there had been times of conflict during the forty-year journey since the exodus from Egypt, the people had learned to trust the leadership provided by Moses, the man of God. After Moses died, the reins of leadership were turned over to a younger man named Joshua. God gave Joshua a very necessary threefold encouragement for the task by saying,

> Be strong and courageous, because you will lead these people to inherit the land I swore to their forefathers to give them. Be strong and very courageous.... Have I not commanded you? Be strong and courageous. Do not be terri-

fied; do not be discouraged, for the Lord your
God will be with you wherever you go.
(Joshua 1:6-9)

## The Intimidating Mantle of Leadership

From my own experience, I can imagine that
young Joshua felt intimidated to be following in the
footsteps of a person who had been as powerful – one
whom he had held in such high esteem – as Moses.
Now it was Joshua's time to lead the children of
Israel to the next step.

I grew up in Mississippi without a father in my
home. In 1964, shortly after becoming a Christian
under the ministry of John Perkins, I became involved with the ministry in Mendenhall and began to
regard Perkins as my spiritual dad. I saw him model
servant leadership in a very wonderful way. John
was a person who, in spite of his third-grade education, displayed all the earmarks of a man of God
whose unselfish leadership would one day enable
him to become the founding president of a holistic
Christian movement that is spreading around the
nation and even into other countries. Naturally I felt
intimidated, as do many second generation leaders
who fear we cannot measure up to the standard established by the current leader.

## Education and Training

After high school, I went on to junior college.
When I talked to John one day in the middle of my
sophomore year, he encouraged me to consider attending a Christian college. We looked at some colleges and found an interesting one in California by
the name of L. A. Baptist College. John worked out a
plan with the coach and the director of admissions to
get me a basketball scholarship. I saw this as fantastic support from a leader who had already done so
much for our community.

## The Need for Finances

After my first year in California, I came back during the summer of 1968 to find a job and stay at home with my family, only to face a pervasive reality. In rural Mendenhall, there were few jobs available for young people, and even fewer jobs for young Black males. After looking for a job for a number of days, I decided to go to Washington, D.C. My brother had told me that he could get me a job there. Two days prior to leaving Mendenhall, John Perkins and I talked about the possibility of developing our own ministry within the community so that young people like me would not always have to leave, but could look at the possibility of having something to which to come back.

With no money, having only a dream and a vision, we started our first summer leadership development program. I became the director. There were three other young people working with me. We offered a Vacation Bible School service to rural churches. The churches opened their doors, and we provided the teaching and all materials at no cost. Little did I know that the process of leadership development was beginning to take place. For me, this project was an opportunity to experience the joy of having a father figure interested in my development as a person. In John's mind, it was doubtlessly a strategic move in grooming my leadership abilities.

## Strategic Leadership Development

Every ministry that wants to survive must pass on the vision to what I call a second generation of leaders. These are the apprentices who will succeed the current leadership and carry the ministry to new heights. Owning the vision is very important because a ministry often dies in the second or third generation if there is not a clear commitment to the original vision. I firmly believe that early on John Perkins, in his role as the first generation leader, wanted me to have a good understanding of the vision for Christian community development.

This became clear as I returned to work in the 1969 summer program. Realizing that racial integration was soon going to come to the public school system, we expanded our Vacation Bible School by adding a tutorial program to provide our youth with adequate reading and math skills with which to face those new challenges. In addition, we added a Black history component because many of our young people did not have a healthy appreciation of who we are and where we have come from. I was given increased responsibility for running the programs.

Having graduated from college earlier that year, I contemplated going to seminary in the fall of 1969. By this time, I had made a definite commitment to be in some type of full-time Christian ministry but still had not made a commitment to return to Mississippi. Understanding first-hand how racism and poverty had debilitated the Black community, my plan as a teenager was to go to college, get an education, and get out of Mississippi as so many friends and family members had done.

A major change occurred in my thinking during May and June of 1970 while traveling with Overseas Crusade, Sports Ambassadors, and Ventures for Victory (a Christian basketball team). We played local teams and shared our faith in Taiwan, the Philippines, and Hong Kong in a missionary effort to use sports to reach the lost. While on that trip, Norm Cook, the coach, observed my leadership skills in dealing with the young Taiwanese and began to challenge me about becoming a full-time missionary under Overseas Crusade or Sports Ambassadors. I thought this was a great idea. I could be involved in missionary work without going back to Mississippi. Yet I responded, "Let's pray and see what God has to say." Six weeks and sixty-plus ball games later, to my surprise, I had to tell Norm that God was calling me back to Mississippi. God kept bringing this plaguing question to my mind: *What is going to happen to the people who are trapped in rural Mississippi if I don't return to help them?*

I returned to Mendenhall after my experience in the Orient and discussed my desire to return to Mendenhall with my future wife Rosie. She agreed that if this was God's call on my life, she would accept it as her call as well. We were married in August of 1970. At the time, I had one year of seminary remaining. Rosie had two years of college to go.

## I Didn't Want to Go Back

After my graduation from seminary in 1971, John Perkins presented me with a huge challenge, "Dolphus, I want you to come back to Mendenhall to work with us. Now, what I need you to do is go out and raise your support." This was another major hurdle for me to overcome. I wanted to get a job and earn a living for my family. I did not want to depend upon other people for my financial needs. Obviously, this was a hurdle God wanted me to face. So after returning to California for Rosie's senior year, we began the process of raising funds. A California church provided more than two-thirds of our support. They helped us to see that God would provide.

## Opportunity to Fail

As indicated above, the summers of 1968, 1969, and 1970 were spent in Mendenhall. The experience was good from one perspective, but bad from another. I learned that the first generation must not only confer a leadership title and responsibility to the second generation, but must also give the power and authority to implement that leadership. It is much more difficult to pass the baton successfully if the leader-in-training has not had an opportunity to fail. John was so interested in my success that he did everything possible to help keep me from failing. However, that approach worked against me. I never had a chance to grow up. I left Mendenhall a boy and came back a boy. Neither seminary nor the summer ministry had provided the kind of training and experience I needed to develop into the seasoned leader who would be ready to lead a growing ministry to our people.

Even after I had been given the responsibility to run all the programs, the first generation leader would step in and make decisions from time to time. This was especially true in areas where he really wanted to see a correct decision made. For example, one time a person was brought in as my assistant and given responsibility over all of the staff. Yet I was not included in any discussion prior to the decision's being made. It was at such points that I felt like I was being treated as a boy rather than a man. Often I felt like going to some other ministry where I could exercise more of my gifts. Today as I look back on the struggles and frustrations, I realize that this was all a part of being a second generation leader. I realize now that it is extremely difficult for a first generation leader to let go. Perhaps, more importantly, no one had given John a road map to follow in developing this ministry and developing a second generation leader. He was going through his own on-the-job training.

## Recommendations

Our experience suggests several recommendations for other ministries which are making long-range plans for leadership transfer. Allow second generation leaders to go away and stay a period of time to gain their own leadership style. Recognize that, more than likely, that style will be different from that of the present leader. However, the first generation must accept that leadership style. The context will no doubt have changed since the founding of the organization. Among other things, the government is always introducing new challenges which affect the way the ministry will be carried out. The ministry will probably have grown in its impact. The backgrounds of the leaders will be different. The second generation leader will have the advantage of standing on the shoulders of the first generation leader.

Many times, first generation leaders view second generation leaders as sons or daughters. At some point the relationship needs to change to that of colleagues and adult peers working together in the service of the Lord. The decision to spin The Mendenhall Ministries off from its parent Voice of Calvary was no doubt made with the best of intentions. However, it came across like a father trying to force his children to grow up. A part of the philosophy was that if the sons failed, they could always come back to their father for help. But because the sons were not involved in the original decision to get spun off, there arose a competitive desire to *prove to Dad* that we were not going to fail. The result was friction between leaders who both wanted to do God's will in serving our communities. Praise God, time and good communication have healed the hurts. Most of the pain could have been avoided, however, if there had been a clear understanding between the first generation leader and the new leader.

So the question is: At what point do we clearly make a transition in our thinking away from feeling like a child and father with its accompanying paternalistic treatment? What is the right time to become partners and start working together? The transition needs to be made first in the thinking process so that it can then be fleshed out better in the action process.

After two decades of leading The Mendenhall Ministries, I am now faced with the same issues discussed above. In many ways, I am now a first generation leader who has come face to face with the same challenges that my mentor had to confront. What to do is not nearly as simple as I used to think. After much prayer and counsel, here are some how-to's I have adopted to assist our second generation leaders in developing their potential:

1. Begin early to give to second generation persons a vision for coming back to the community.

2. Provide leadership opportunities for second generation persons to grow and to develop.

3. Encourage second generation leaders to go to some other place to work for one to three years in order to gain a greater sense of their own leadership skills and potential.

4. Allow second generation leaders to grow without looking over their shoulders all the time. Demonstrate confidence in emerging leaders as they begin to work in the ministry.

5. Agree to talk openly and often. One of the worst things that could happen would be not enough communication and affirmation occurring in both directions.

Apprentice leaders need a lot of affirmation from the incumbent leader. One byproduct of Christian humility on the part of leaders-in-training is often a measure of insecurity regarding how their work is evaluated by the current leader.

It is important for the life of the vision that the organization should work to grow new leaders. New individuals coming in can take hold of the vision and can do a great job of pursuing it. A fantastic way to grow vision and commitment is to begin early to shape the second and third generations. A lot of my leadership development took place haphazardly. I learned from the first generation as I went along. And that is fine. But there also needs to be more structure to pull it off. Joshua, the leader-to-be, no doubt observed Moses in many different situations. But it was a totally different experience when Joshua took over the reins and had to be the leader himself. It was certainly very different for Dolphus Weary to take up the leadership reins from John Perkins. Smooth transitions can be achieved by:

1. Both parties sitting down and agreeing on the way the transition will take place.

2. Following that plan once you have agreed upon it.

3. Regular affirmation and an expression of commitment on the part of each person.

After the transition, the first generation leader should not be "kicked out" completely. Nor should he hang around and stifle the second generation, who needs a certain amount of space in which to grow. A partnership relationship should be formed so that the former leader knows that he can make recommendations to the new leader. The new leader must also know that he has not only the freedom to make decisions, but also the freedom to go to the first generation for advice – as well as the authority to decide whether to follow that advice.

I learned a number of things from my experience over the last twenty years:

1. Leadership is not easy for either the first generation leader or the apprentice leader.

2. It is easier to analyze how things should have been done than to do everything right on a day-to-day basis. I like the one-liner which says, "When you are up to your armpits in alligators, it is difficult to remember that your original objective was to drain the swamp."

3. Nobody gave our pioneers a manual on leadership development. They had to create their own rules as they went along. It is a credit to their reliance on God that they have done so well.

4. Leadership training should be a more prominent part of college and seminary programs. This should include how to develop apprentices as well.

5. Problems can help in your development, even as the Bible says in James 1 and as Clarence Walker points out in his chapter on "Man Wounds" in this book.

6. It is important for the second generation leader to express what his expectations are, too, so that there can be a meeting of the minds on important issues. Differing unspoken assumptions can lead to confusion.

7. The first generation leader is more open to suggestions than we sometimes think.

# 7

---

# Sound Management in Church Women's Groups

by Delores L. Kennedy-Williams

*Delores L. Kennedy-Williams, M.S., D.Humanities, is completing eight years as international president of the Women's Missionary Society of the African Methodist Episcopal Church. She leads management, leadership training, and motivational workshops around the world. She is the author of many articles, including* How to Win and Keep Members, Pornography and the African American Family, Do We Really Want Younger Members?, *and* How to Organize for Success.

The Women's Missionary Society of the African Methodist Episcopal (AME) Church has thrived as an organization since its inception in 1894. Our purpose is:

1. To help women and youth grow in the knowledge and experience of God through Jesus Christ;

2. To seek fellowship with women in other lands by initiating and maintaining a support system that will enable all to achieve fulfillment; and

3. To make possible opportunities and resources to meet the changing needs and concerns of women and youth through intensive training, recruitment, and Christian witnessing.

An international organization, our current membership is approximately 800,000 women, girls, and males from age two to twenty-six.

## Problems

When I was elected president, I noted some characteristics of the Women's Missionary Society which could be improved.

First and foremost, we were having severe management problems which could be attributed, in part, to a lack of administrative procedures and little or no use of management as a tool.

1. There was no distinction made between staff and line officers. Both groups are elected by the same body. However, the president was charged with the responsibility of general supervision.

2. The organizational structure was complex and did not lend itself to good communication.

3. There had historically been little clarity of command. Many who held office did not know to whom they reported and from whom they should receive direction, especially when there might be differences of opinion. Directives of the administrative committee and the executive board were routinely ignored.

4. There were no provisions for removing officers or members who refused to follow the directions of the leaders charged with that responsibility.

5. Budgetary needs of the national organization were met, or not met, depending on the mood of the persons on the regional board who were to forward the funds. Yet, those persons continued to have full voice and vote regardless of their lack of financial cooperation.

It is difficult for people to change a tradition. Nonetheless, if African American church women's organizations are to achieve their full potential as we move toward the twenty-first century, it is clear that we cannot continue to operate an organization on emotion. Rather we must put into place sound management techniques. Strong measures must be taken. Change cannot be seen as the enemy, but rather as a means to achieve our goals. The fact that Black social and civic organizations have moved ahead swiftly by making use of all that has been made available gives reason to believe it is possible in church women's organizations as well.

## Hypotheses

As part of my graduate study, I took a formal look at the question of management of church women's groups. Three hypotheses (guesses to be tested formally) were posed to explore what corrective actions would be required in such organizations. In order to evaluate the hypotheses, questionnaires were given to 175 people who attended a convention of the National Council of Negro Women, which brings together thirty-three unrelated Black Christian and secular women's organizations. My hypotheses held up.

### Hypothesis One

The first hypothesis was that *severe management problems are being experienced in Black church women's organizations because there are no administrative procedures in place, and management is not used as a tool.* The findings were revealing:

1. The average length of service for leaders of church groups was two years compared with an average of three years for secular groups. This is a significant difference of 50 percent.

2. All the church women leaders expressed frustration with a system that seemed to resist change and which, at the same time, expected so much of them.

3. In most instances, the current administrations did not enjoy good working relationships with the previous administrations and sensed little continuity.

4. Each church leader worked between 60 and 70 hours per week. All of them received what is considered a full-time salary, but which is not intended to be comparable to like secular positions.

5. There were no written job descriptions for any of the positions. There were no educational requirements. No job training was provided by any of the organizations.

6. There were no procedures manuals in any of the church organizations.

7. There was little or no staff.

8. In all the Black church women's organizations, line officers and staff officers were all elected.

9. Consequently, the leaders voiced frustration with trying to get the job done without having the power of hiring, demoting, or firing.

10. Only one of the organizations had a headquarters. None of them had procedures for storing permanent records. In most instances, the office was the kitchen table of the current president.

11. The annual budgets of the Black church women's organizations averaged $300,000.

12. Financial accountability is being pursued aggressively by only a small number of the organizations. Two of the organizations had recently changed procedures for receiving and disbursing funds to be on a par with other well-run national associations. Another organization is still operating under a very archaic financial system, and change is being resisted heartily.

In two organizations, the bonding agency has issued a warning that surety bonds will not be renewed until they come into compliance. Neither the secular Financial Accounting Standards Board nor the Evangelical Council for Financial Accountability considers it prudent for a single individual to be responsible for receiving funds, depositing them, and reconciling the bank statement. Yet this was still being done in some instances.

By comparison, the United Methodist Women and secular groups were almost completely opposite the Black church women's organizations.

1. The length of service was about the same, and the president was also overworked.

2. However, the United Methodist Women's president was a volunteer, assisted by a paid professional staff of thirty-five. The deputy general secretary was the staff person. There was clear delineation of staff and line positions.

3. There were detailed job descriptions and a comprehensive procedural manual.

4. Workshops were held regularly for staff and for volunteers to train them in proper administrative procedures.

5. The secular organizations most often added the former leader to the board of directors, from which vantage she brought continuity without introducing a sense of competition.

### Hypothesis Two

The second hypothesis was that *thriving non-profit, non-church-related Black organizations which experience fewer management problems have administrative procedures in place and make use of management as a tool.*

The questionnaires and interviews supported this hypothesis.

1. The average length of time in office for the national presidents was three years. The hours worked per week varied from four to forty-eight, with thirty being the average. None of the presidents was paid a salary, though all their expenses were reimbursed.

2. Without exception, the organizations all had a headquarters, an executive director as the paid staff person, and a staff large enough to get the job done. Change was generally well received because guidelines were established in advance. The first year of most new administrations was seen as a year of transition.

3. The immediate past president of each of the organizations served as a member of the executive board and was not viewed as a threat or a thorn because she continued to work at uplifting the organization.

4. All of the organizations had detailed job descriptions and procedural manuals.

5. All records were kept at headquarters. No property of the organization was spread here and there. They did not have the checkbook in one place, the historical documents at another place, and the awards received at still another place.

6. Procedures were in place for every branch of the organization, from the national level to the local level. There was no confusion about who reported to whom and when.

7. There was also clarity as related to budget obligations and – unlike the church organizations – local and regional organizations were required to support the national body to remain members in good standing.

Respondents from Black church women's organizations indicated that Christian character is the most important criterion in selecting their leadership. Education was second. Organizational skill was ranked seventh out of nine choices.

Black church women's organizations were often locked tightly to tradition, were not overly interested in selecting leadership based on training for the position, and seemed to equate *any* post-high-school training as "preparation." Thus, one who possesses a master's degree in elementary education is seen to be "qualified" and "prepared" to manage a half-million dollar budget, even though she may have had little training or experience in finance.

Respondents from the United Methodist Women and those from secular organizations similarly chose character as the most important criterion. Education was also second. In both cases, organizational skills followed. Professional history was ranked fourth, but was next to last among the Black church women's responses.

### Hypothesis Three

The third hypothesis was that *personalities play a larger role in performance satisfaction in Black women's organizations than in White women's organizations.*

This hypothesis likewise was upheld as well. The United Methodist Women respondents indicated very little by way of personality playing a large role in staff performance satisfaction.

## Analysis

The day when one could assume an office of responsibility and expect to be an expert simply because one is being led by the Lord Jesus is over. Unfortunately, the libraries of new books relating to general church management and administration do not touch on the management of international lay organizations within the church. Massey and Johnson acknowledge that the women's missionary society is the most powerful group in the Black church. Yet they devote but one paragraph to the management of such groups. Leaders will have to avail themselves of the available literature and adapt it to fit their individual needs.

Massey and McKinney (p.78) stress the importance of the Black administrator having or acquiring the wisdom to create a machinery (management as a tool) that is conducive to the development of harmonious working relationships with the mixed bag of personalities which they are called to lead.

Peter Drucker maintains that the executive organization is expected to get things done correctly. However, in Black church women's organizations, effectiveness is absent much of the time. Drucker observes that there seems to be little correlation between a person's IQ and effectiveness. Being an effective executive comes through training and hard work.

It appears that many Black church women's organizations are not open to change and frequently will make life difficult for those leaders who insist on making changes. Drucker emphasizes the importance of facing change:

> An organization which just perpetuates yesterday's level of vision, excellence, and accomplishment has lost the capacity to adapt. And since the one and only thing certain in human affairs is change, it will not be capable of survival in a changed tomorrow.

Mark Pastin acknowledges that there are many hard problems to be faced by those who manage. New insights will not be achieved until the manager is willing to admit that the old tools do not work. That is not as easy to do as it is to say because it involves risk.

The manager who dares to operate outside the box of old tools risks offending the old toolmakers and, if not that, certainly runs the risk of accepting the challenge of shopping for new management tools. It is the fear of failing that keeps many of us – particularly women in a male-dominated arena – from moving out of the comfort zone.

There is general agreement among writers of management manuals, church administration technique manuals, and effective executive how-to's that the organization – whatever its goals – will not live well nor long unless a well-planned, well-executed agenda is in place. Larson maintains that churches are dying for lack of leadership. He feels churches need a strong dose of what he calls "Madison Avenue 'stuff'" (p. 9), techniques that almost anyone could learn in a beginning management course. The Women's Missionary Society, like the church, is our Lord's business, and should be run – in many respects – like a business, but a redeemed one, to be sure. For instance, many of the suggestions made by the authors of this book represent sound business approaches. In addition, let me list some others:

1. The organization should be accountable to a representative board of directors which takes its constituents' interests seriously. In addition to following the teaching of the Bible, this board needs to operate on the basis of what may be called good business principles.

2. There should be clear lines of accountability for each staff person in order to minimize confusion.

3. A written job description should detail the limits of each employee's responsibility and authority.

4. A up-to-date manual should prescribe normal operating procedures of the organization.

5. There should be adequate separation of duties to ensure accountability in financial matters.

6. Annual audits should be performed and reported to the membership in a timely fashion.

These are just a few of the many good business principles which are transferable to the church women's organization context. Yet most of our leaders, like much of the church in general, have little or no business training.

Further, Larson maintains, the four P's taught in any basic marketing class are very important: Product, Place, Promotion, and Price. Too often administrators in society (and in the church) are not clear on what the product is, where the place of our calling is, how we should promote our product, and what price we are willing to pay.

Dickens and Dickens's study confirmed that Black managers are keenly aware that in order to survive in the White corporate world, there are some interpersonal skills they have to learn that are approached differently in the African American culture. One such skill involves confronting another person successfully regarding an issue about which there is some conflict and finding a way that mutual agreement can be obtained. The desired result is for action steps to be developed and implemented in an appropriate time frame.

One reason Black managers need to apply more effort in this area is cultural. The African American culture tends to operate in a more personal, relational manner. On the other hand, White culture seems to operate in a more depersonalized, organizational manner. As a result, Blacks tend to take disagreement more personally. This factor supports the third hypothesis, that personalities play a much larger role in performance satisfaction in Black church women's groups than in White church women's groups.

We would do well to adapt a page from Kanter (1989). He notes that American corporations have moved from the premise that if you don't own it or control it, it might hurt you and should be treated like the enemy. Times have changed. Corporations now look for ways to network for increased cost-effectiveness and efficiency. As one example, Ford Motor Company has forged more than forty coalitions with outside commercial entities. Another example is the "Pooling, Allying, and Linking (PAL)" across suppliers which has produced a variety of advantages for Digital Equipment Corporation, including cost savings, quality improvements, early access to new technology, and the capacity to develop new components without having to make everything in house.

Why should they have all the fun? PAL can become a viable option for Black church women's organizations. If, for example, just the AME Women's Missionary Society, the CME Women's Missionary Council, and the AME Zion Women's Home and Foreign Missionaries would network on a program to train female prisoners to become computer literate, funding would be available and many more persons could be served. But first we must learn to be "PALs" and not to worry about which organization controls.

Much of the literature confirms the importance of putting administrative procedures in place and the importance of training our leaders to become managers.

## Evaluation

What should a leader be expected to do? To inspire? To motivate? To educate? To innovate? To lift? To heal? To guide? To direct? Is she to be a prophetess? A promoter? A promulgator?

Among those who responded to the questionnaires, there was a wide difference of opinion on
many topics; such as, the criteria required to be effective leaders, the importance of tasks performed by the
chief executive officer, what a leader should be able to
do, what a leader is expected to do, what a leader is
called to do. Whatever the answers, the leader must
administer and exercise all responsibilities in an or-
derly way. Otherwise, severe problems will occur (see
1 Corinthians 14:40). The implementation of sound
management practices is not an appendage to the
mission of Black church women's organization, but
is biblically rooted in its very nature as noted else-
where in this book.

Leaders of Black church women's organizations
have an obligation to lift the constituency's level of
consciousness on the use of sound management as a
tool. Each of the organizations has stated purposes
and goals. These should be placed within an appropriate management system. We have all received
God's orders and God's gifts. We must now find a
system in which to use them effectively.

Black church women's organizations must begin
to create a climate to train people to change the system in meaningful ways. The constituency must
likewise be receptive to innovation. A well-managed
institution is healthier. The time is now to move from
chaos to community. It is not easy to change attitudes, but it is possible. The women who are
members of these organizations deserve excellence in
administrative-managerial leadership.

Black women's organizations must begin to move
away from personalities and deal with principles. It
is always appropriate to attack a person's process
when that process appears to be inconsistent with the
stated goals and purposes, but it is never appropriate
to attack the person. African American church wom-

en's organizations must become familiar with the three most common management principles and make them an integral part of their groups:

1. Delineation of authority – Who is responsible for what? Who has the authority to act?

2. Clarity of command – Who reports to whom and who takes direction from whom? This becomes increasingly important when there are differences of opinion.

3. Accountability – Does everyone understand what is expected? Who is accountable for achieving results? Much energy is wasted on arguing this point when it is not clear. Thus, there will be less energy left to focus on the goals of the organization.

Black church women's organizations need to become familiar with Dickens and Dickens's five-stage confrontation model. This will assist them in realizing that conflict is not always negative and that conflict can be transformed to serve the organization and the individuals who experience conflict:

1. Approach – Bring up the subject in disagreement in a direct, but tactful, manner. (Involve only persons who are part of the problem or part of the solution.)

2. Impact – Express your interpretation of the issues to the other person. Share feelings, attitudes, and opinions about the issues. (Avoid discussing personalities.)

3. Penetration – Penetrate the other's feelings, attitudes, and opinions. This stage is used primarily to narrow the focus of the conflict so that only the facts involved in this particular issue are being discussed. Do not dredge up old, unrelated issues at this time.

4. Follow through – Be as logical and objective as possible. Be less emotional.

5. Closure – In the closure stage, seek mutuality. Discuss areas of agreement. Agree on mutually acceptable action plans.

## Implementation

Consistent with the ideas presented above, some years ago seven historically Black denominations came together under the umbrella of The Congress of National Black Churches. These denominations realized that together they could be more effective on many issues than if they operated separately. Even before Kanter espoused her theory of PAL, those denominations began to put into place several meaningful programs to assist the communities which they serve. They have Project Spirit, a tutorial and training program, operating in many Black churches around the nation. They have a fellowship program which provides financial assistance to enable many Black seminarians to receive training that otherwise might not be attainable. In addition, they have more recently begun to offer a training program for financial management in the Black church.

While this organization has begun to meet many needs, it is my feeling that the women's organizations of those denominations ought also to come together and explore programs and projects which we can pursue jointly.

## Recommendations

The preceding discussion leads naturally to a series of recommendations:

1. The officers of the AME Women's Missionary Society, the AME Zion Women's Home and Foreign Missionaries, and the CME Women's Missionary Council should consider planning a joint retreat to begin to explore ways to Pool, Ally,

and Link (PAL) ourselves. One early project might be joint sponsorship of a management training series for all our officers.

2. Each of the Black church women's organizations should appoint committees or hire outside persons to prepare procedures manuals for every phase of the organization.

3. Each should develop complete job descriptions for every position in its organization.

4. Each should clearly separate line positions from staff positions and should change job descriptions to reflect same.

5. Each should give serious thought and training to stewardship development. Endowments and economic development programs will enable the organizations to invest more in their mission programming.

6. Black church women's organizations should cease to think of themselves as competitors and begin to empower one another. For example, if the CME Women's Missionary Council has an outstanding hunger program in a city, the AME Women's Missionary Society does not need to duplicate, but should rather assist, that program. The same is true of other programs and other denominations.

## Changes We Have Made

For our part, after nearly eight years of struggle, we have produced a procedures manual, hired a full-time office manager who doubles as bookkeeper, and hired two part-time secretaries. We have developed job descriptions, put into place a management system, and eliminated in-fighting between staff and line officers.

We have completely computerized our offices, with
networks established between the president (who re-
sides in a remote city and travels extensively), the
treasurer, and headquarters. The resulting
increased efficiency has freed me from being an office
manager to being an advocate for the people who
elected me to serve as their president. Not only have
these changes brought about unprecedented
opportunities for improved effectiveness, they have
also transformed my assignment from a wearisome
chore to a welcome calling.

## References

Dickens, Floyd, Jr., and Jacqueline B. Dickens. *The
Black Manager.* New York: Amacom, 1982.

Drucker, Peter F. *The Effective Executive.* New York:
Harper and Row, 1966.

Kanter, Rosabeth Moss. *When Giants Learn to
Dance.* New York: Simon and Schuster. 1989.

Larson, Philip M. Jr., *Vital Church Management.*
Atlanta: John Knox, 1977.

Massey, Floyd, Jr., and Samuel B. McKinney.
*Church Administration in the Black Perspective.*
Valley Forge, Pa.: Judson, 1976.

Pastin, Mark. *The Hard Problems of Management.*
San Francisco: Jossey-Bass, 1986.

# 8

---

# African American Leaders: Women on the Front Line

## by Sherry Sherrod DuPree

*Sherry Sherrod DuPree, Ed.S., A.M.L.S., M.A., is a college reference librarian and lecturer. DuPree is chair of the Florida Library Association's Religion Caucus and chair of the Rosewood Massacre Forum, a group dedicated to preserving Black history. DuPree has authored eight books, among them:* Biographical Dictionary of African American Holiness-Pentecostals 1880-1990. *She is co-author of* Exposed! Federal Bureau of Investigation (FBI) Unclassified Reports on Churches and Church Leaders.

The seeds of a vibrant Christian movement were planted in the hearts of our ancestors during the slavery era. Some slave masters taught a selective Christianity as a means of controlling the slaves. Other White Christians risked everything to carry the true message of the gospel to the Black man. Records from the era indicate that the slaves, though largely illiterate, were able to discern where the slave masters were modifying the message to use it as an instrument of control. Of particular interest to the slaves were the parallels of American slavery to the account in Exodus. Their sermons and lyrics show that liberation theology engaged the slaves' minds as hardly anything else could.

Following Reconstruction, Black families moved from the plantations of the South to the industrial North in large numbers, lured by the growing numbers of jobs available in the factories of Detroit, Chicago, New York, and other cities. Wages were low; so the men often took two jobs, with the result that they were able to spend very little time at home or in the church. Women, therefore, were forced to assume leadership at home, in the church, and in the community.

### Re-examination of the Scriptures

African American men and women are re-examining the Scriptures because of changing social patterns in the church and society. They note that the Pentecost event was an outpouring of the Spirit along with the gift of prophecy for both men and women (Acts 2). Further, Ephesians 5:21-33 teaches mutual submission where the loving, sacrificial self-giving of the husband corresponds to the submission and respect enjoined of the wife. First Corinthians 7:3-5 stresses partnership between men and women rather than a hierarchical relationship. Decision-making by husband and wife is to be by mutual agreement.

Other items of interest include the tradition of women as prophets and judges in Old Testament Israel and Peter's announcement of the priesthood of all believers. Equality is stressed again in Galatians 3:28, "There is neither Jew nor Greek, slave nor free, male nor female, for you are all one in Christ Jesus."

### Order in the Church

The church is ordered by the spiritual gifts given by God (1 Corinthians 12). These gifts are given to both men and women. Thus, Spirit-filled women and men should be free to exercise all spiritual gifts.

According to the Bible, the woman was created from the man and for the man. The man is to exercise leadership and authority over the woman. Both  will be fulfilled when they reflect the pattern that God desires. (See Genesis 1-3.)

There is lack of agreement regarding the assertions in 1 Timothy 2:8-15 and 1 Corinthians 11:3-6; 14:34 that women are to be silent in the church and are not to teach or exercise authority over men. First Peter 3:1-6 and Ephesians 5:22-23 teach that wives should submit to their husbands. In addition, the credentials for male elders and deacons in the church are stated in 1 Timothy 3:1-10. The traditional denominations stress that women pastors and elders clearly violate God's order for the church. Those denominations which interpret these passages literally do not allow women to participate at the upper levels of leadership.

## Women as Followers

African American women serve as evangelists, missionaries, teachers, preachers, money-raisers, and church planters. But often after a pioneer work matures, positions of power become more formalized; and men tend to take over the positions of leadership. This is true of such denominations as the Church of God in Christ, the largest Pentecostal trinitarian church, which has never allowed women pastors.

Such denominations stress the importance of hierarchy in the relationship between men and women. Supporters of this position cite the lack of women priests and kings in Old Testament Israel. They note that the twelve apostles were all men. They also refer to New Testament passages 1 Timothy 2:8-15 and 1 Corinthians 11:3-6; 14:34, as noted above. In these denominations, women can be evangelists. Under special conditions, they have been allowed to pastor in some denominations. For instance, if a husband dies

and the widow can maintain the church membership, she may serve as interim pastor until a male
pastor can be appointed.

## Women as Leaders

At the same time, more and more women are
serving as pastors. The African Methodist Episcopal
(AME) Church, the oldest Black denomination, and
many of the Spiritual, Holiness, and Pentecostal
churches were the first to use women in pastoral
leadership roles.

The United Holy Church of America, the oldest
Pentecostal body (founded in 1886), and The Pentecostal Assemblies of the World (founded in 1907) were
two denominations that accepted women with certain
constraints. Discrimination was present at the upper
levels. Women could serve as pastors and ministers
but not as bishops. Women could attend the bishops'
council but they could not speak. They were required
to write notes to the council leader, who would respond if he wished. Otherwise, the women were
ignored.

## Documenting Great Leaders

More than any group in this country other than
Native Americans, our people must overcome obstacles which are systematically put in our path. One
such obstacle concerns the omission and distortion of
the significant contribution of Blacks to the history of
America and of the world in general. A concerted
effort is required to collect, organize, archive, and pub-
lish our true history.

One of the roles of the historian is to uncover and
document events and present them so that our people
can see that we are descended from noble, faithful
people who have shown their mettle and succeeded
against all odds. In addition to the usual written and
graphic records, recognized oral historians (*griots*)

are veritable walking encyclopedias. These griots – your grandparents, the elders at church, community elders, and so forth – need to be interviewed now in order to formalize the information that has heretofore been passed along in the oral tradition.

The history of the African American church has survived because of various publications by churches, colleges, and church educational institutions, to say nothing of denominational publications.

**FBI Files: A New Research Source**

The Freedom of Information Act has allowed access to a new source of historical information on American citizens. From its own files, we see that the Federal Bureau of Investigation (FBI) has been leery of African American religious leadership for decades, primarily because of the fire and conviction it injects into the people. Leadership influences from the church and college campus pose a "threat" to the status quo of American economic and political society. African American church leaders were often discredited in a calculated effort to cut off the head so that the body of members would not function effectively.

Women included in the FBI files include Ida Robinson (1891-1946), whose radio broadcast was first rescheduled and then suspended because she made comments about the Japanese during World War II. Leaders from many persuasions were monitored and attacked by the government, suggesting that no person is safe from unwarranted federal observation and intervention.

Can you imagine what other files one might find at the Central Intelligence Agency (CIA) and other government agencies? Many church leaders see their ministries as including the uplifting of both the spiritual and the temporal lives of their congregations. Some leaders are actively addressing social injustices as part of the civil rights struggle. The government monitors church leaders to sense the level of unrest in the community.

## Political and Human Rights

The AME Zion Church provided prayer and financial support for Harriet Tubman (ca. 1821-1913) and other outspoken male and female advocates for freedom. Other Black and White churches, including Quakers, Methodists, Mennonites, Baptists, and Lutherans cooperated to help make a way to victory by providing Tubman with a network of people and hideouts for the underground railroad to the North and to Canada.

The AME Church supported Ida B. Wells-Barnett (1862-1931), who became a crusader against lynching, poor housing, and discrimination. Her leadership against lynching turned out to be strategic. No Black man would have been permitted to lead such a campaign at that time. As a woman, Wells-Barnett was able to garner support from some Whites as well as from African Americans.

## Today's Women Leaders

Some of the reasons that leadership is becoming more inclusive today in African American churches are as follows:

1. Women are more visible in important roles. Consequently, positive attitudes toward women are developing. In my church, women are used in lay leadership roles during worship service – helping at the altar, helping with the offering, and videotaping the church services.

2. Women are enrolling in seminary and college in record numbers. They are writing term papers and dissertations on African American religion and related subjects. Therefore, accurate,

documented, detailed information will be more available in the future.

3. Churches are reaching out in new areas such as the singles ministry, which is composed mostly of women. The director of Christian education is usually a woman. Women start, operate, and are the majority of participants in most neighborhood Bible study groups.

Many traditional denominations have a number of female leaders. At the same time, some women are establishing non-denominational churches because of barriers they encounter. These women are networking to share their mutual concerns about gender discrimination in the church. These women operate small churches. Some are pastoring only younger members in cases where older members have difficulty accepting a lady pastor. In *The Black Church in the African American Experience,* C. Eric Lincoln and H. Mamiya estimate that less than five percent of the clergy of historic Black denominations are female. There are, proportionately, more Black women clergy than white women clergy.

## Acceptance of Women Leaders

Many Black, White, and integrated denominations which were previously closed are now allowing women in the roles of pastor and bishop. For example, in 1986, Eva Burrows was elected as commanding general of the Salvation Army. Soon after, in 1989, Barbara Harris, an African American, was elevated to bishop of the Episcopal Church's Diocese of Massachusetts.

A number of denominations were organized with women accepted as pastors from the outset. One example is the Church of God (Anderson, Indiana) which was organized in 1880 and which is predominantly White. Another example is the Mt. Sinai Holy

Church, which was founded by Ida Robinson, a Black woman. The largest number of women in pastorates today is in the integrated United Methodist Church.

At the same time that the number of women pastors and bishops is growing, the reverse is true in the Pentecostal Assemblies of the World (founded in 1907), a predominantly Black group. The women are usually pastors of smaller congregations.

Among the Black Baptist denominations, the only one favoring ordination of women is the Progressive National Baptist Convention (organized in 1961). The other Baptist groups are divided on the issue. Some regional bodies allow women as pastors. However, the national organizations have not taken a stand for women.

Men are accepting these women. One pastor told me that she preached from the floor level for two months at the beginning of her pastorate. The transition to the pulpit in the third month was smooth as a result. The men continued to attend and support the church. The women and men felt closer to her because she did not push her authority. Another pastor always wears a robe in the pulpit over her street clothes in order to show leadership and not to draw attention to herself.

**Women and Education**

The various Methodist and Baptist churches have been in the forefront in providing a college education for women as well as for men. Education is playing a prominent part in the preparation of women for leadership at a time when fewer men are going on to seminary. One reason some men give is that they can make more money in other professions. One said that his father had been a pastor, and their family was never sure of finances from week to week. He didn't want his family stressed in this way. He would share his religious views as a lay member.

On the other hand, Black women are entering and graduating from seminaries and colleges in record numbers. Many of them are over thirty-five years old. Many have grandchildren. They are stable and concerned about meaningful change in society. The shortage of men active in the church has forced women to accept leadership roles. These women are forming networks and exchanging ideas for growth. They are preparing themselves to minister professionally, not only as pastors and teachers, but also as hospital chaplains and administrators, to name a few.

A major milestone occurred when Mrs. Deon Yvonne Walker Taylor was inaugurated as president of Wilberforce University in 1984, the first woman president of any college related to the AME Church.

Historically, responsibility for the education of church members and for personal counseling was often given to Black women by men who did not have the skills and/or time for these ministry areas. As a result, women have been ministering to youth, senior citizens, and other women for years. These women support prayer groups, serve as mentors, and encourage members to seek God for strength. They use as biblical role models Mary, Hannah, and Esther.

## Mentors and Role Models

Our youth can benefit from emulating positive role models, such as Rev. Bernice King and Yolanda King, daughters of Dr. and Mrs. Martin Luther King, Jr. Self-confident, poised, and warm, Bernice delivered her trial sermon in 1989 from the pulpit of the historic Ebenezer Baptist Church, where her father and grandfather had also preached. Yolanda King is an aspiring actress and owns her own business. The offspring of parents who were also leaders, these women are future leaders. Our young women would do well to model themselves after such

women. Some may say they need someone whom they
know to be their mentor. In that case, they may observe leaders in their church and select a mentor
who is closer to home. They must always remember
that the best mentor is Jesus Christ.

Reading is also important for growth. The best
book is the Holy Bible. In addition, take time to read
some of the works of Christian female authors.

## Conclusion

Each Christian has the responsibility for taking
the initiative in promoting dialogue between men and
women Christians. An effort should be made by both
men and women to involve and not reject helpful
leadership.

Christian leaders – men and women – must resolve to teach sound doctrine and to lead in worship
which glorifies God. For most of the twentieth century, Black women have not been recognized as leaders in mainline denominations, except in their own
prayer meetings, evangelistic groups, choirs, and
mission agencies. On the other hand, women have
always been successful in exercising leadership in
non-traditional churches: pastoring, planting congregations, even starting new denominations.

Today, more and more Black women are successfully discharging leadership and decision-making
roles as they express their God-given gifts in all areas
of the church. Yet, the question about appropriate
roles for women remains controversial.

Even as the church wrestles with what to do with
aspiring women leaders, another problem promises
to grow even larger as we enter the twentieth-first
century. The sheer number of women entering the
workforce is leaving the church without many of the
volunteers who used to sustain church activities.

The environment in which our members and our neighbors live is increasingly more complex than it used to be. The African American church must respond with more programs customized to reach its various publics: youth, people with AIDS, unwed mothers, single parents, senior citizens, and so on. Black women, with or without a license or ordination, continue to minister to such needs at all levels in the church.

## For Additional Reading

Bedell, Kenneth. B. *Yearbook of American and Canadian Churches.* Nashville: Abingdon, 1993.

DuPree, Sherry Sherrod. *Biographical Dictionary of African American Holiness-Pentecostals 1880-1990.* Washington, D.C.: Middle Atlantic Regional Press, 1989.

DuPree, Sherry Sherrod. *The African American Holiness-Pentecostal Movement: An Annotated Bibliography.* New York: Garland, 1995.

DuPree, Sherry Sherrod, and Herbert C. DuPree. *Exposed! Federal Bureau of Investigation (FBI) Unclassified Reports on Churches and Church Leaders.* Washington, D.C.: Middle Atlantic Regional Press, 1993.

Greenberg, Blu. "A Crime Against God," *New York Times (Late New York Edition),* 12 July 1994, A19.

Hine, Darlene Clark, Ed. *Black Women in America: An Historical Encyclopedia.* Brooklyn: Carlson, 1993.

Murphy, Larry G., J. Gordon Melton, and Gary L. Ward. *Encyclopedia of African American Religions.* New York: Garland, 1993.

Payne, Wardell J., ed. *Directory of African American Religious Bodies: A Compendium by the Howard University School of Divinity.* Washington, D.C.: Howard University Press, 1991.

"President Bush Praises King, Hears Pointed Comments from Minister Daughter, Bernice," *Jet,* 3 February 1992: 4.

*Progressions, A Lilly Endowment Occasional Report: The Black Church in America,* Vol. 4, Issue 7, February 1992, 14-15.

Smith, Amanda Berry. *An Autobiography: The Story of the Lord's Dealing with Mrs. Amanda Smith, the Colored Evangelist, Containing an Account of Her Life Work of Faith, Her Travels in America, England, Scotland, India, and Africa as an Independent Missionary.* Chicago: Meyer, 1893.

Tate, Mary M. Lewis. *The Constitution, Government, and General Decree Book of the Church of the Living God, the Pillar and Ground of Truth.* 2d ed. Nashville: The New and Living Way Publishing Co., 1924.

"That New Time Religion (Ordination of Woman Bishop B. C. Harris)," *National Review,* 10 March 1989: 16-17.

Townes, Emilie, "Ida B. Wells-Barnett: An Afro-American Prophet," *The Christian Century.* 15 March 1989, vol. 106, 285-86.

# 9

---

# Leading a Small
# Christian Business

by Melvin Banks

*Melvin E. Banks, Sr., M.A., Litt.D., was the founding
president of Urban Ministries, Inc., in 1970, and now
serves as chairman and chief executive officer. The
company is the leading African-American-owned
producer of Christian education products designed
for all African American churches and denominations, including Sunday school and Vacation Bible
school literature, books, and videos.*

It was my privilege to be the founding president of
what eventually became known as Urban
Ministries, Inc. (UMI). My concern for the
spiritual welfare of African Americans can be traced
to my childhood in Birmingham, Alabama. Shortly
after receiving Jesus Christ as my Savior I was in-
vited by the person who led me to the Lord to share
my testimony in a street meeting on the outskirts of
Birmingham. When I finished my little testimony,
an old gray-haired African American man strolled
up, complimented me on my testimony, and in the
short conversation that followed, quoted a Bible verse:
"My people are destroyed from lack of knowledge"
(Hosea 4:6a).

Unbeknownst to this gentleman, the Holy Spirit
used that verse to quicken my heart to the need of

communicating a knowledge of God's Word to African Americans. I pledged in my heart that I would dedicate my life to that task. Of course, at that early age I didn't have the faintest idea how that would be accomplished.

Later in life, while working at a predominantly White Christian publisher, the opportunity came to begin the fulfillment of this boyhood dream of disseminating the Word of God by means of the printed page. When I was elected to serve as president of UMI, in many respects I was unprepared to run a business. Up until that time, my focus had been on "ministry" as I conceived of it – teaching Sunday school, working in youth groups, and serving people without the necessity of planning and organizing the work of others. I remember one of the board members advising me, "Mel, now you will have to shift your focus from ministry to marketing and running an organization."

Only after some hard trials, errors, and additional training did I come to appreciate the basic principles so vital to creating and developing an organization which could have longevity. I share them here with the prayer that others endeavoring to serve the Lord by operating a business may find them useful.

### Establish a Mission Statement

Among the lessons I have learned about running an organization, perhaps none has been more helpful to me than one I did not discover until UMI had been operating for about three years. The lesson was the crucial importance of establishing a mission statement for the organization.

Why is it so important?

A mission statement forces an organization to decide what it really is all about. Having established what it really wants to do, the organization can devote its energies to pursuing the mission and not become sidetracked in many nice activities which may be good, but which do not enable the organization to accomplish its purpose.

Until the mission statement was developed, we each operated on the strength of our own unexpressed, individual understanding of what we were about. Our board, however, wisely encouraged me to sit down with the staff and wrestle through why we existed, what we really believed the company was all about, and what we intended to pursue.

After a few weeks of reflection and dialogue, we arrived at what we felt was a cogent statement of the UMI mission. The board of directors provided additional input and finally approved the following statement, which we then posted in a conspicuous place in our office for the benefit of both our internal staff and our external customers:

> We are called of God to create, produce, and distribute quality Christian educational products, and to perform Christian educational services which will empower God's people, especially within the African American community, to evangelize, disciple, and prepare persons for serving Jesus Christ, His Kingdom, and His Church.

Every word was carefully chosen to express what we believe the organization is all about. While we recognize that the statement may be changed as the company evolves and grows, yet until we prayerfully and deliberately change the mission, it is our focus, the plumb line by which all activities are evaluated and approved.

## Share the Vision

Few things can be accomplished single-handedly. It takes the help of others. That is doubtless one of the reasons God said of Adam, "It is not good for him to be alone." God knew that Adam could not do all that the Creator wanted him to do if he had to do it alone. So God provided him a helper (Genesis 2:18). In the same way, we need the help of others if we are to accomplish goals in our organizations. One of the crucial ways of securing the help we need is to include others in the vision of what we want to accomplish.

My wife was the first person with whom I shared the vision of what later became UMI. I understood early on that if this new venture was going to be a success my wife and family would have to buy into it. Not only was this important for my own emotional well-being; but as it turned out, our entire family has been deeply involved in the success of the company.

In the development of this embryonic idea, one of the first things I endeavored to do was to get the reaction of people I thought could benefit from a publication written with African American young people in mind. I spoke with a number of pastors, youth leaders, Sunday school teachers, and students to see if they agreed with me that such materials were needed. When I discovered that people were wholeheartedly in favor of African-American-centered literature, I discussed the vision with key people I thought could constitute a board of directors for such an organization. This group of advisers has been invaluable in shaping and directing the vision God placed on my heart.

Through the years, we have found it necessary to continue sharing the vision. Internally, I have found it invaluable to dialogue with the staff concerning plans in order to get their input on ideas that I think should be explored.

Some leaders disdain discussion about their plans. Usually it is because they are insecure. They fear others may belittle or tear them apart. Some are arrogant, convinced others could not possibly improve on what they say God has given them. In my opinion, people who do that make a grave mistake. I have found that by discussing my vision and plans, others can improve on my ideas. Sometimes I may abandon my ideas altogether when I become convinced that others have better ones. I figure I can always evaluate the advice and adopt the best. Having listened to others, I can then use my best judgment. Oh, the wisdom of listening to what others have to say!

Additionally, we find it necessary to share our vision with pastors and other Christian education people, with investors, bankers, suppliers, and the public at large. Obviously, one has to be selective in what is discussed with whom, but the need to inform others of what God has placed on your heart cannot be minimized.

During Jesus' stay on earth, He repeatedly discussed His mission with others. In one of the most notable instances, He quoted to the people at Nazareth the Old Testament passage which outlined His mission:

The Spirit of the Lord is on me,
    because he has anointed me
    to preach good news to the poor.

He has sent me to proclaim freedom for the
    prisoners
    and recovery of sight for the blind,

to release the oppressed,
    to proclaim the year of the Lord's favor.
    (Luke 4:18-19)

Other statements by the Lord reflect His vision for this church age:

... On this rock I will build my church, and the gates of Hades will not overcome it. (Matthew 16:18)

... This gospel of the kingdom will be preached in the whole world.... (Matthew 24:14)

Therefore go and make disciples of all nations, baptizing them in the name of the Father and of the Son and of the Holy Spirit, and teaching them to obey everything I have commanded you.... (Matthew 28:19, 20a)

The vision of our Lord has engaged the church for some 2,000 years. But had He not shared it, we never would have known what it is and never could have bought into helping to accomplish it, albeit imperfectly.

**Establish Goals**

One of the most helpful seminars I ever attended was conducted by Tom Skinner and Stanley Long under the rubric of "Time Management." That's where I discovered the crucial importance of goals, priorities, and strategies.

Without engaging the perennial debate over the distinction between a "goal" and an "objective," let it be said that a company must establish what it wants to accomplish. (According to some, "objectives" define long-range unmeasured pursuits, whereas "goals" define short-range measurable pursuits.) While the mission statement identifies in a general sense what the company will be about, the goals and objectives of the company will state what the company intends to accomplish – whether short- or long-range.

One of the established objectives of UMI has been the development of Sunday school literature contextualized to the needs of African Americans across denominational lines. We settled on this objective because (1) there was a clear need for such materials as reflected in surveys we conducted and our own observation, and (2) we were convinced that predominantly White Christian publishers would never jeopardize their larger established White market by integrating their materials to satisfy the needs of African Americans. Even now, some twenty-five years after the development of UMI's Sunday school curriculum, the attitude of most publishers appears to be the same: some occasional token representation, but no serious attempt to relate the Scriptures to the concerns of African Americans.

Establishing an objective and sticking with it is very important to an organization. It goes without saying that serious thought has to be given to establishing objectives because time, energy, and scarce resources must be allocated to pursuing these ends.

At UMI, we constantly look at several areas in order to establish or revise objectives:

1. Program: WHAT are we going to do and by WHEN?
2. People: WHO is going to do it?
3. Place: What SPACE and EQUIPMENT do they need in order to be successful?
4. Price: What will it COST, and where will the money come from?

## Determine Priorities

Not long ago I picked up a pamphlet in which a small new organization had listed some forty goals it intended to pursue. Certainly the organization will have trouble reaching that many goals. And even if it tried, its energies would be so scattered that it may reach none of them very well. The reality is that no organization can achieve all the objectives it can come up with in a brainstorming session. So the goals have to be prioritized. That is, the organization must determine which goals are most important to be tackled at a given time and in what order. In addition, it is critical to identify which goals must be eliminated entirely.

## Develop Strategies

Strategies are the methods the organization will use to reach the goals. In developing strategies, the resources of the organization must be taken into account. What are the strengths of the people who will be doing the work? If we don't have people with the needed strengths, can the missing resources be obtained somewhere else? Do we have the space, money, and so forth?

## Be Persistent

If there is one principle which I have found more needful than all the others, it would have to be the principle of sticking with the task. I have seen many worthwhile projects started, only to be abandoned after a few months or a few years. Of course, one can become convinced that what he or she thought was a worthwhile project is wrong. But more times than not, people become discouraged because things don't progress as fast as they think they should; so they give up a perfectly good project.

This principle was brought home vividly to me when UMI had been going about four years. I was discouraged – very discouraged. One morning in my devotions I was agonizing in my spirit to the Lord, asking Him why He gave me the responsibility for leading UMI.

"Don't You realize I don't have the skills or money needed to make this company succeed?" I was angrily confessing to the Lord.

At that moment the Lord spoke to me in a way which I had never experienced before. The voice echoed throughout my whole being, "I did not ask you to do this because I thought you were so skillful. I chose you because *I thought* you would stick with it."

The emphasis on the past tense, *"I thought,"* conveyed to me that if I decided to give up, God would choose someone else. In response to Him I answered, "Lord, the least I can do is be faithful." I have never regretted that decision. Since then, I have never again entertained the idea of giving up on what I am convinced God has called me to do.

# 10

---

# Always Work Yourself Out of a Job

by Beverly Yates

*Beverly Yates is a Registered Professional Nurse. Married for 43 years, she and LeRoy Yates are founding members of Westlawn Gospel Chapel of Chicago and founders of Circle Y Ranch Bible Camp. Beverly served twelve years as president of the Chicagoland Christian Women's Conference. She has written articles for* Interest Magazine.

September 1960 was an exciting, memorable time in our family life as it became time for our first-born son to enter kindergarten. LeRoy, Jr., (we called him Butch) was tall and well built for his age. I was delighted to be able to say finally, "Yes, my son goes to school." But we were also experiencing the fears and tears of separation anxiety as the time drew near to take him to school. There was no Headstart program in those days, and we couldn't afford nursery school. This, indeed, was Butch's first day of school. (You might say that he was even better prepared for this momentous occasion than we were.)

Mason, the school he was scheduled to attend, was only three blocks from our apartment. Shortly after our arrival on the appointed day, we were informed of a last-minute boundary change to eliminate overcrowding in that school. The principal told us to register our son at Corkery School, about ten blocks from our home.

Needless to say, a number of parents were upset about the change, but we all went immediately to the adjacent neighborhood school, an imposing three-story, red brick fortress-looking building. We will never forget the image of Miss Brown, the White principal, blocking the school entrance, refusing to register our children in her public school. This incident was a real introduction to blatant racism, Chicago style. It was difficult explaining to our son and his little friends why they could not attend school that day.

This confrontation caused me to resolve to join the PTA and to become involved in as many activities as possible in this newly integrated school. At that time, I knew our child's best protection from being lost or mistreated in that hostile atmosphere was an involved mother.

Joining the PTA surely was my ticket to the D. J. Corkery Elementary School. The principal, Miss Brown, quickly learned our names and became open to those of us who attended meetings and provided assistance to teachers and students.

The Chicago Region PTA was very strong and effective in the sixties, holding classes and conferences on a regular basis. In a short time I attended PTA training courses and became an officer, even president of our local school PTA, for a number of years.

Serving in PTA while our four children were in elementary school gave me my first insight into the gifts of leadership I had within me. I tasted the power and influence of becoming a community leader, and it was good!

The PTA manual said that "A good leader is always working himself out of a job!" The PTA by-laws supported this principle by calling for annual elections with a term of office being for one year. An officer in the PTA could only serve two consecutive terms in the same office. In this way, no one could take permanent ownership of any position as we sometimes see in our churches and Christian organizations where one person holds office "till death do us part!"

Through sharing important responsibilities, we become aware of the gifts and talents of others in the unit. We also learn the important principle that no one is indispensable. In Exodus 18:17-23, we see how Jethro advised that great leader Moses regarding his leadership of the children of Israel in the wilderness. Moses was burdened with the people and their problems, trying to do all the leading himself until Jethro showed him a better way:

"What you are doing is not good. You and these people who come to you will only wear yourselves out. The work is too heavy for you. . . . You must be the people's representative before God and bring their disputes to him. Teach them the decrees and laws, and show them the way to live and the duties they are to perform. But select capable men from all the people – men who fear God, trustworthy men who hate dishonest gain – and appoint them as officials over thousands, hundreds, fifties, and tens. Have them serve as judges for the people at all times, but have them bring every difficult case to you; the simple cases they can decide themselves. That will make your load lighter, because they will share it with you. If you do this and God so commands, you will be able to stand the strain, and all these people will go home satisfied."

In summary, Jethro advised Moses to:
1. Choose capable people

2. Train them
3. Organize them
4. Delegate work to them
5. Hold them accountable

Jethro's advice is appropriate for us; and it works. Confident leaders learn to share authority and are not afraid to allow others to make mistakes. Good leaders rejoice when their associates do a good job and are generous with applause. First Corinthians 12 substantiates the need for and the use of God-given gifts within the body of Christ. In *Using Spiritual Gifts,* R. Wayne Jones says:

> The Body of Christ, therefore, is the arena in which we discover the will of God and who we are in Him. When we discover the spiritual gifts for carrying out His will we have in a real way become the Body of Christ. The church, then, should be a laboratory for discovering God's will and the gifts that He exercises through us. The church community, therefore, is to be a gift-evoking community.

Wouldn't it be a wonderful sight to see the local church alive with everyone's gifts being discovered, developed, and displayed?

I love to sing "To be Used of God." The happiest times in my life are when God is using me where I am needed most. I assume that other believers in Jesus Christ feel this way, too. So when I learn their gifts, I try to plug them into an area of service where they can grow best.

I remember how organized we were when I was in the high school band. That experience helps me realize that a good leader is like a good band director, who:

1. Discovers people's abilities;

2. Places them in the right section;
3. Teaches them;
4. Practices with them; and
5. Advances them so that one day they may lead.

## Leadership Transfer Within the Family

When we met in 1948, my husband-to-be was just beginning his college studies. His desire to become a doctor impressed my young heart, as did his exceptional good looks. Before he could complete pre-med, however, he was inducted into the Army. A new Christian, LeRoy served in the medical corps on Korean battlefields for more than a year.

The experiences God led him through in Korea convinced him of God's calling, not to medicine, but to the ministry. LeRoy obeyed and followed the Lord. I followed my husband. Together we have been involved in local church development, Circle Y Ranch Bible Camp, and the Chicagoland Christian Women's Conference for more than thirty-five years.

Through these ministries we have been involved in, and exposed our five children to, the life of becoming servants for Christ.

Today, all our children are saved and committed to serving the Lord in their vocational lives. Our oldest son, LeRoy, Jr., is a physician, practicing obstetrics with skill and prayer. Jonathan, our youngest son, is a computer systems manager. Both young men are married and have children of their own. We have three daughters, who have made their mother's heart glad. Mary is married and is employed as an officer in a Dallas, Texas, bank. Joyce is a busy working mother with two beautiful children. Sara, our youngest daughter, is a college student.

When we first became involved in the Lord's work, we prayed that God would give us wisdom and help us to not lose our own family to Satan as we worked to help others. God is faithful – none of ours are lost.

## A Vision for the Future

Seventeen years ago, Circle Y Ranch Bible Camp needed an executive director. My husband resigned his job as a microbiologist to assume leadership of the camp. The need for someone to manage the kitchen soon became apparent to both of us, and within a year I resigned from nursing and became food service director, or head cook, at the camp.

Little did I know how much God would teach me about Himself, about others, and about myself. The camp kitchen taught me the true meaning of servant-leadership as we worked from sunup to sundown, preparing three meals a day for more than one hundred people.

Marie Campbell is one of the fine women who worked consistently with me for several summers. She volunteered three or four weeks of her vacation each year to cook at Circle Y. I shared with Marie my knowledge of the kitchen, which other good cooks before had taught me. She learned my technique for making rolls. I finally caught on to bread-making. (Marie makes the world's best onion bread.)

Marie and I confided personal problems with each other and prayed together for our children. LeRoy and I supported Marie through the death of her son and again a few years later when her dear husband went to be with the Lord.

Marie has replaced me as food service director at the camp. She retired from her job with the state of Michigan and moved into one of the houses on the campsite. She attends workshops and classes on food service. She does a very good job working with and training young people as kitchen staff so that the camp will never be without good cooks.

Look around you. God has someone with the appropriate gifts and talents that you can begin training to do your job. When you allow another person to do what you enjoy doing, you practice the art of dying to self, killing jealousy, and hiding envy behind the cross. God never asks us to give up anything without having something better for us.

When we hang on to what we should release to someone else, we never find out what that "better thing" may be. May God help us leaders to find ways to work ourselves out of a job.

## Reference

Jones, R. Wayne. *Using Spiritual Gifts.* Nashville: Broadman Press, 1985.

# 11

---

# Building a Team

by Russell Knight

*Russell Knight is the founding president of Chicago Urban Reconciliation Enterprise, Inc. He is an experienced youth worker and consultant and is the author of* Take 5.

A t one time, immense changes in technology demanded that America move from transportation by horse to a new mode of travel called the automobile. At the beginning of this new experiment, many supporters of the faithful horse were not easily convinced. They knew the worth and value of the horse, but the automobile was a brand new concept.

The style of pastoral leadership in the African American church, going back even into the period of slavery, has almost always been dictated by the times. An enslaved people and those recently liberated required a "take charge" leader. For that reason, the predominant type was an authoritarian "Moses" to lead his people to the promised land.

As the pastor, he was the one who possessed the vision, spoke for his people and the community, was an outstanding orator and preacher, was seemingly a magician in administrative matters, and for the most part, operated within the realm of selective accountability. That simply meant that the pastor was a law unto himself and could only be held accountable as he chose to allow himself to be.

Whole congregations grew to be totally dependent upon an individual who, during the slavery and post-slavery eras, has been described as perhaps the most essential person in the African American community. The importance of the Moses type of leader cannot be minimized. This style of leadership was highly successful and should be credited in large part with the survival of a people in the midst of severe crisis.

Whatever the critics may say, it is doubtful that African Americans would have accomplished as much without the vital leadership provided by these godly, and often legendary, men. It is interesting, nevertheless, that even though the church was born and developed in the New Testament, supporters of the Moses style of leadership almost never use the New Testament to justify that style. They go instead to Old Testament leadership models that predate the church. This is reasonable since the slave church equated its struggle with that of Israel in the Old Testament. In that context, Moses spoke for God and carried the vision.

In order to fully comprehend the "Where are we?" question, we must at least acknowledge that after the civil rights era, many changes began to take place in the African American church, just as many changes began to transpire in society at large. One of these changes had to do with the increased education and competency level of the laity. No longer was the pastor the best educated individual in the community and the church. Better job training and better positions in the workplace slowly helped create lay persons who were highly skilled in the very things that were formerly done at the church by pastors. The outside community began to look to others as spokespeople for African Americans based on their competence to speak intelligently on a wealth of topics.

More and more, on their jobs, African Americans were trained to manage people, set budgets, hire personnel, advertise, raise funds, build buildings, and coordinate programs. Not only this, but in many churches, laymen were also attending Bible schools and seminaries in order to enhance their lives spiritually. Soon, it became obvious that biblical knowledge was not something that only pastors could pursue.

While in many quarters charisma alone seemed enough on which to get by, other pastors struggled to find ways to lead such enlightened memberships. Churches began questioning the concept of a Moses-style leadership and started trying to find whether or not something called "team" might be more applicable to today's African American church.

In fact, newer congregations have already begun exploring the idea of multiple leadership (two or more pastors or other staff). They are no longer looking to find "a" pastor who preaches, teaches, visits, counsels, administers, manages, and speaks for his congregation. Believing that all churches have several members with pastoral gifts, they are prepared to encourage more leadership at the top.

The question of "Which kind of leadership style is needed in the church today?" is not a criticism of what happened successfully in the past. The question is whether that which worked in the past will carry us through the difficult days ahead, or do we need to encourage a different style – one which will better meet our needs while releasing for service many of the laymen in our churches who are severely underused.

Today's church must have leadership with a holistic view of mission and the gifts to answer some of the social ills of our communities as it continues to evangelize. Therefore, more and more church leaders are participating in community development projects and working on such problems as housing and jobs.

Under the style of leadership that we call "team," the senior pastor is much more of a team player and coach. This does not mean that there is no longer a place for "the buck to stop," but it does mean that we can no longer have one individual who feels obligated to make independent decisions that impact others. The new "player/coach" is not intimidated by differing points of view or differing personality types. In fact, he understands that this can be a great advantage in team building.

Many congregations continue to call pastors who can provide them with a Moses style of leadership, while others feel it necessary to try something different. I see this desire for change as a positive direction for many churches, but I don't think that every church has to move immediately to the new while the old still works.

One of the oft-stated criticisms of the Moses style of leadership is that it does not easily embrace change. Newer churches recognize that ways must be found to reach the unsaved and unchurched, which may include such matters as helping them to find work and restoring to some a sense of dignity and worth.

Successful churches will eventually investigate the concept of "team" and stop asking an individual to pastor in the traditional sense of the word. They will recognize the fact that no one man can give them all that they desire and need in leadership.

Jethro advised Moses that it would be wiser and more effective to use a team in the accomplishing of the ministry. Moses did the right thing. He listened, and the results were outstanding. It is important to see that Moses had some of the same negative conditions that today's church leaders face. He had to contend with murmurings and conflict (Exodus 16 and 17), and yet he succeeded. Once he learned how to organize and use the abilities of others, the ministry prospered.

Although the church certainly is not a business, it must be more businesslike in its operation. In the concept of "team," excellence is promoted, accountability is enlarged, ownership is shared, and creativity is encouraged, thereby enabling the entire church to make better use of natural leaders.

It is important to note that there are few models of "team" leadership in the African American church at this point in time. Those who defend the Moses style of leadership have the weight of tradition on their side and use it to almost deify what worked in the past. While I, too, agree that it was invaluable in its time, that style of leadership blocks the development of other leaders and, therefore, denies the church a total concept of leadership.

Churches that choose to try the team approach to leadership will find it difficult to learn from others. Most people have only been exposed to one style of leadership in the church, so the models of other styles are few or non-existent. We are desperately in need of those who will pioneer a new way, who will become models to churches which anxiously look for better ways to encourage leadership development. So, simply asking the question, "Where else is this being tried?" does not solve the problem.

Without a doubt, the concept of team leadership is biblical. *Moses* developed a team, *Jesus* used a team to accomplish his goals, *Elijah* selected *Elisha* to help him, and *the early church* enlarged its team to reach its goals.

Today's leaders must not attempt to lead individually or in isolation, nor should they be obsessed with empire building. Instead, God is looking for leaders who will humbly serve as part of a team which supplements and encourages one another. This kind of team, fully accountable, can mobilize the church in the days ahead.

In order to create an effective team ministry, the following suggestions are valuable:

## Mission and Purpose

Many churches and para-church organizations have a difficult time identifying their mission and purpose. However, it is important to be able to start right if you hope to end right. Actually, by answering two very simple questions, you can discover your organization's mission and purpose. Those questions are (1) What will we be doing? and (2) Why will we be doing it?

As a consultant to churches, para-churches, and small businesses, I have found that it is not uncommon for the answers to these two questions to be hazy and unclear. Even though there is a mission or purpose statement in the constitution or charter of an organization, few who are connected know what those documents actually contain.

The *process* that creates the mission statement is as important as the actual answers to the questions. In other words, it is critical to have the right people in the room when the mission statement is being formed and that they all have something to do with creating what everyone can "own."

When an organization has a clear mission statement which comes from contributions by everyone in the group, the entire team will be motivated around this "vision." However, when the mission is passed on by the boss, board, or a limited subset of those who have a vested interest, then there is often a problem in motivation and ownership.

While staying at the Hampton Inn in Colorado Springs, the most prominent thing I saw posted at the registration desk and in the elevator was the mission statement of that organization. I was impressed with the quality of the service I received there. The management informed me that the entire hotel staff had participated in the process of forming the mission statement.

It is a good idea to find ways of constantly reminding everyone on the team of their mission and to have periodic evaluations which tell how you are doing.

Finally, it becomes necessary every now and then to update these statements. With the passing of time and the changing of leadership and personnel, it is not unusual for missions and purposes to change. It is important to stay current.

## Team Member Profile

Develop a desired profile for discussion with potential team members. Once again, in order to have the right people on the team, it is important to include many others in the process to ensure leaving no stone unturned.

First, *compose a list of tasks* which must be performed by the team. By grouping this list according to those that are related, you will arrive at several team work categories based on what must be done.

## Gift Discernment

Finally, design a tool for finding out *what potential team members bring to the team.* Here you are looking for gifts, skills, talents, and areas of expertise. You can tell the strength and weakness, as well as the needs of the team, by evaluating this information periodically. Future vacant positions should also be filled only with team input.

Often churches make the mistake of equating good managers with good leaders. These are related, but separate, gifts. One is not superior to the other. However, it is unusual to find one person with both gifts. A healthy team concept does not demand that an organization find someone with both.

## Recruitment and Hiring

When seeking to build a team it is important to select future team members based on their training, gifts, skills, talents, and whatever else they bring to the business, ministry, or agency. In other words, it is critical that there is a solid match between the individual and the task.

While recruitment may be in the hands of one individual, the actual hiring of a team member should not be limited to just one individual. Large organizations usually have a department that is charged with the hiring procedure. In smaller operations, it is advisable to have two or three people involved.

Most larger operations have a written procedure that is called an orientation or *entrance procedure.* I recommend that even smaller operations put their procedures in writing.

The actual final decision to add to the team should involve the *employment application, several interviews, and background investigation.* Again, use several persons in the process.

As early as possible in the procedure, it is important to place an *information packet* in the hands of the prospect in order to guarantee that as many of his/her questions have been answered as possible prior to the initial interview. In addition to information about the organization, this packet should include a *tentative job description, information on salary and benefits, evaluation procedure, conflict resolution procedure, and "exit" procedure.*

It is becoming increasingly common for organizations to make use of a hiring tool called a *personality profile* to help match the individual with the task and with the other members of the team. Experts tell us that a person's personality style influences his or her leadership style. A caution to observe in the use of various employment tests: God helps us enhance our strengths and minimize our weaknesses. There is no way to test for this impact.

## Ideas That Work in Team Building

Finally, here are a number of suggestions that can lead to effective team building.

1. Check the previous work record of the applicant by contacting past employers. Look for problems and negative trends.

2. A positive work environment is essential in building a unified team.

3. In order to know the needs of your team, it is important to ask and not assume.

4. Excellent timely communications will eliminate most problems.

5. Practice "catching people doing things right" and reward team members regularly.

6. Encourage creativity and problem-solving. Give credit where credit is due.

7. As often as possible, interview both the prospect and his or her spouse. Doing so can be quite revealing.

8. Servant leaders must possess humility in abundance.

## For Additional Reading

Engstrom, Ted W., and Edward R. Dayton. *The Art of Management for Christian Leaders.* Grand Rapids: Zondervan, 1987.

Peters, Tom. *Thriving On Chaos.* San Francisco: Harper & Row, 1988.

Rush, Myron. *Management: A Biblical Approach.* Wheaton: Victor Books, 1985.

Van Fleet, James K. *The Twenty-two Biggest Mistakes Managers Make & How to Correct Them.* Englewood Cliffs, N.J.: Prentice Hall, 1986.

# 12

---

# "Man Wounds": God's Process for Developing Successful Male Leadership

by Clarence Walker

*Clarence Walker, Ph.D., is president of Clarence Walker Ministries. An ordained minister, he is a marriage and family therapist in private practice. Walker is author of* Biblical Counseling with African Americans: A Ride in the Ethiopian's Chariot.

As a counselor who works with individuals as well as couples, I have begun to understand the wounds and scars that people experience from childhood through adult life. I have especially come to understand and be empathic regarding the emotional wounds received by African American men. There is probably no group in this nation that is more wounded. However, they are often left to suffer in silence because men are socialized to be strong and macho.

We are not supposed to show emotions or vulnerability since this is viewed as a sign of weakness, and we are supposed to be tough and able to take it. We are not supposed to cry when we are hurt or, for that matter, even admit when we are hurt. I have discovered in my therapy with Black men that they will often cover up their emotional hurt with anger; thus their hurt may manifest itself in domestic and other forms of violence and rage. They may also try to drown the pain with alcohol and drugs. Finally, some deny their pain altogether. Moreover, even when a man acknowledges his woundedness, very often he puts the blame for that hurt on the Black woman. It has been the experience of this counselor that the most devastating wounds inflicted on men are not from Black women, but rather those they sustain from other men, especially Black men.

Of the African American men I see in therapy, 85 percent are born-again Christians from various denominations. Since a large number of them are in ministry of some sort or another, there is a need for them to see the connection between their "man wounds" and God's plan for leadership development in their lives. This chapter briefly addresses the issue of "man wounds" as it relates to African American men, especially Christians. It is my hope that it can be used to generate discussion among Black Christian brothers regarding their wounds, their past baggage, and current emotional issues. Further, this chapter can also enlighten the reader on how God may be using these wounds to make them into men of God and effective Black leaders. With that in mind, I shall proceed to define "man wounds."

## "Man Wounds" – Four Kinds

Man wounds are hurts experienced by men in their relationships with other men. There are four kinds: familial wounds, communal wounds, vocational wounds, and collegial wounds.

The first and often the most impacting are "familial wounds," hurts which we experience in relations with the male members of our family of origin – our father, grandfathers, brothers, stepfather, stepbrothers, uncles, and cousins.

"Communal wounds" are abuses that we receive from men of the larger community in which we grow up:

1. The next door neighbor who does not like us.
2. The bully who picks on us.
3. The gang which beats us up.
4. The Black boys who tease us and take us through the humiliation of "The Dozens," where our mothers are called degrading names.
5. The club that excludes us and won't let us join.
6. The sports team that won't let us play.
7. The male school teacher with whom we have an adversarial relationship.
8. The local policeman who may have it in for us.
9. The local bigots who put us down.

"Vocational wounds" encompass the hurts we experience from male employees and supervisors, to say nothing of the wounds we experience when we are passed over for a desirable job.

"Collegial wounds" are those we experience from friends, associates, and close work colleagues.

If ever there was a man who understood these four sets of man wounds, it was Joseph, the eleventh son of Jacob.

## Joseph's "Man Wounds"

Any one of these sets of hurts can be emotionally devastating, but Joseph was a man who, by the grace of God, triumphed over all four. First, he became the victim of familial wounds. The wounds he experienced from his brothers were the results of wounds they had experienced from their father:

When his brothers saw that their father [Jacob] loved him [Joseph] more than any of them, they hated him and could not speak a kind word to him. (Genesis 37:4)

Joseph's brothers were offended by the preferential treatment he received from Jacob. The Bible says:

An offended brother is more unyielding than a fortified city, and disputes are like the barred gates of a citadel. (Proverbs 18:19)

We can see here an example of how man wounds are generational. Jacob, the father, was simply repeating with his children the legacy of rejection that he had experienced from his own father: "Isaac . . . loved Esau, but Rebekah loved Jacob" (Genesis 25:28).

## Generational Patterns

A generational pattern of men hurting men in this family is now set. Although he had intended no harm, Jacob's father, Isaac, had shown a lack of acceptance of Jacob. Subsequently, Jacob shows a lack of acceptance for Joseph's ten brothers. Jacob had been hated by his brother Esau (Genesis 27:41). Jacob's son, Joseph, was hated by his brothers. This scenario is typical of many of the Black men I see in therapy. They are among the victims referred to in Exodus 20:5-6, which states that the sins of the father are visited on the children even to the third and fourth generation. Wounds from fathers frequently lead to wounds by brothers. The reason for this is that in some respects the father has more impact than the mother in the family. Proverbs 17:6 says, "The glory of children are their fathers" (KJV).

The Hebrew word for *glory* may also be translated *ornament*. Therefore, fathers are the ornament of their children. In the Old Testament context, ornaments were symbols of identity, security, authority, and piety. So, today, fathers are living symbols of identity, security, authority, and piety.

Many African American men are guilty of "parental Ichabod"; for the glory of the children has departed. The children lack identity and security and in many cases do not respect authority; for mothers are to be symbols of love and nurturance, whereas fathers are to be symbols of authority. When fathers are absent (or present but uninvolved), mothers become the symbol of authority by default. Thus, in the Black community we have many women overfunctioning while many men are underfunctioning in the role of authoritarian. Mothers who should be gentle, loving, and nurturing, in many cases, are perceived to be hard and tough. Of necessity, they must fill the roles of both mother and father. Paradoxically, many of those mothers who are able to function successfully as both authoritarian and nurturer often confuse the children by virtue of that success. African American male children in such environments sometimes develop a love-hate relationship with the parent who is present – generally the mother – as they are unable to express their anger directly against the parent who is absent, the father. This often develops into intense power and control struggles between the mother and her male offspring.

Boys who are reared in a female-headed household often cease relating to the mother as a symbol of love and nurturance. They sometimes view their mother – correctly or incorrectly – as controlling, domineering, and man-acting. In many such cases, the male children rebel, trying to prove their manhood by competing with the mother for power. In their hearts, they surmise that it is a male and not a female who is supposed to be the "man of the house."

Hence, many males rationalize that they should take the absent father's place as the man of the house. They become parentified children – assuming parent-like responsibilities. Their rebellion becomes an attempt to differentiate themselves from their mother, who, of necessity, is discharging the dual roles which have fallen to her. Their actions are a way to make a behavioral statement, "I am the man, Mother, not you." All of this is set in motion by the father's not being present, or being present but uninvolved.

When the father is present but overfunctions in authority, the result is resentment. The proper balance of support, discipline, and limit-setting creates respect for the father. The overuse of discipline or the imbalance between discipline and support often creates resentment in the children that leads to rage. This is why the Bible says, "Fathers, do not exasperate your children. . ." (Ephesians 6:4).

Moreover, neglect and rejection also create great anger in Black male children. It is my opinion that a father's rejection is more negatively impacting than that of one's mother. This has to do not only with the role of males as fathers, but also with men in general and the position they occupy in the plan of God:

. . . A man . . . is the image and glory of God; but the woman is the glory of man.
(1 Corinthians 11:7)

Were it not for the admirable job done by the African American mother for the last several hundred years, the plight of our people today would be sad indeed.

## Man as Image Bearer

Man was created to reflect God's image. When my opinion suffers, it is one thing. When my image suffers, it is another thing altogether: my reason for being suffers. My purpose suffers. To be hurt by a man, thus, is to be hurt by someone who should reflect the image of God to me. When Joseph's brothers were hurt by their father, they experienced their deepest man wounds not only because of Jacob's relationship to them as a fellow man, but also because he was the one who should have been most zealous in looking out for their welfare.

Since the man represents the image and the glory of God, man wounds impact me as though I have been hurt by God Himself. If my father abandons me, it is like God abandoning me. If a male abuses me, it is like God abusing me.

These issues often continue in a man's life and are projected onto other male authority figures, most notably their pastors. (Oftentimes, the same issues a male church member had with his father may be repeated with his pastor because pastors represent a man's second opportunity to be "fathered.")

## Man's Roles

Males can often occupy five critical roles in the family. First there is the *savior*, the glue that holds the family together. Second, the *rescuer*, the referee in family fights. This role is usually assumed by the father or older brother but can be any member of the family.

Third, there is the *villain*, the bad guy, the one the others hate but who usually has power in the family. Fourth, there is the *angel*, the good person who seems to do no wrong, the recluse, the eccentric, quiet one who stays to himself. And, finally, most families have a *black sheep*, one who feels no one loves him, who feels abandoned, put down, and abused.

A thin line separates the villain from the black sheep. The differences are in the areas of power and respect. The villain is often feared and even reverenced openly but resented secretly. The black sheep, on the other hand, feels powerless because he is not respected by the family.

Joseph occupied multiple roles in this regard. He was the angel to his father and the villain to his brothers. Given the treatment he received from his brothers, there were times when he no doubt felt like the black sheep. Early on, Joseph added salt to the wounds their father had inflicted on the ten brothers by sharing his dream with them:

> Joseph had a dream, and when he told it to his brothers, they hated him all the more. (Genesis 37:5)

But in God's perfect timing, Joseph became the savior of his brothers. God often intervenes in families by giving some special ability or knowledge to the family's rejects in order to bring balance. I have seen instances where this person later becomes the salvation of the family in a time of crisis.

## Dehumanization and Victimization

Being part of a family of wounded males, it was highly likely that Joseph would experience wounds from various ones of them. First, they criticized him behind his back. Next, he became a victim of their verbal abuse, ". . . they hated him and could not speak a kind word to him" (Genesis 37:4). Finally, when the occasion presented itself, they took serious advantage of him:

> So when Joseph came to his brothers, they stripped him of his robe – the richly ornamented robe he was wearing – and they took him and threw him into the [empty] cistern. (Genesis 37:23-24)

In what seemed to be a cruel twist of fate, Joseph became the victim of physical abuse at the hands of his blood brothers. Were it not for Reuben, they would have killed him even as Cain had killed his brother Abel. The brother-against-brother syndrome occurs frequently in Black families, often resulting in tragedy or even the murder of one male member by another. Spike Lee captured this problem vividly in his movie *Jungle Fever* where a father killed his own son. A tragic real-life example of this in our time is the killing of singer Marvin Gaye by his minister father.

Many of these disputes can last for years, even a lifetime. So here we have Joseph – young, alone, alienated, isolated – the victim of familial man wounds. His problems were just beginning, however, as he was to become a victim of the second type of wounds: hurts from men of the larger community, or "communal wounds."

> So when the Midianite merchants came by, his brothers pulled Joseph up out of the cistern and sold him . . . to the Ishmaelites, who took him to Egypt. (Genesis 37:28)

Joseph was alone when he heard the camels coming. No doubt he was excited, expecting to be delivered from his pit, only to have his hopes dashed. These Midianite men who could have rescued the young Joseph, who could have been his liberation – these men of the greater community who could have become his heroes – only compounded Joseph's pain.

Being treated like human cattle is the history of Africans who were sold by other Africans to White merchantmen who treated them worse than property. Many Black brothers are still carrying on the legacy of the Midianites and selling their fellows out to the system, to our racist Caucasian brothers. Instead of being safe havens in a stormy sea, these men collude with the oppressors for personal gain and help keep their own brothers in bondage. These Midianites are found in positions of political, economic, and even ecclesiastical leadership.

In addition, a large number of Caucasian males continue to behave like the Ishmaelites and continue to enslave, use, and abuse Black men for their racist, materialistic, self-aggrandizing agendas. More unfortunately, this legacy is also present in the ranks of evangelical Christendom, in spite of the fact that more and more leading ministers are speaking out against such attitudes and practices. It is heartening to note that the Promise Keepers movement is actively fostering more Christian attitudes between the races.

Joseph has now experienced familial and communal man wounds. The journey continues with "vocational" wounds as Joseph is sold by the Ishmaelites to Potiphar, an Egyptian officer, head of Pharaoh's executioners. It is at this point that we get a first glimpse into God's plan of leadership development. The Bible says:

> The Lord was with Joseph and he prospered. . . . When his master saw that the Lord was with him and that the Lord gave him success in everything he did, Joseph found favor in his eyes and became his attendant. Potiphar put him in charge of his household, and he entrusted to his care everything he owned. (Genesis 39:2-4)

The key phrase is that the Lord was with him. Rather than complain about his unfair treatment at the hands of the men of his family and community, he made a decision to grow where he was planted, to make the best of a bad situation, and to turn a demeaning circumstance into a prosperous one. Too many Black men want to simply play the blame game – blaming the White man, their parents, the system. But blaming will not cause us to become victorious. What we must do as Black men is to complain less and commit more, to protest less and invest more. We must learn as men to look for and make the best use of the opportunities available to us. Empowered by God's presence, we must be men of integrity, prayer, diligence, faithfulness, hard work, excellence, and character.

## Challenges, Challenges

Promotion brought with it a new set of challenges for Joseph. The first challenge was how he would respond in his new environment. He came to Potiphar's house as a servant slave and was elevated to overseer, a great testimony to his ability to take a lemon and make lemonade.

The second challenge, however, was even more formidable. Joseph was tempted sexually and propositioned frequently by Potiphar's wife. The issue of sexual immorality is destroying many otherwise-successful Black men in the secular as well as in the religious world. Being a true man of spiritual integrity, Joseph resisted – not because his master's wife wasn't desirable – but because of his commitment to his God. He asked her "How then can I do such a wicked thing and sin against God?"

Joseph was the victim of sexual harassment on the job by none other than his master's wife. Too many Black men fall after achieving success because they are not temperate enough to resist one or more women in their environment. Thus, sexual immorality destroys their effectiveness. Sex becomes the hex that kills their leadership potential.

When Joseph resisted the temptation, he was falsely accused of rape by the woman who had tried to seduce him, causing him to be put in prison by his boss. As head of the executioners, it seems that Potiphar would have had Joseph executed if he had believed his wife's story. Potiphar was saving face. He knew Joseph's character; and, no doubt, he knew his wife.

Thus Joseph was wounded this time by his male superior, a man for whom he had worked hard, for

whom he had been completely loyal. He had given his
all to help his master achieve success. The result? He
was thrown in jail for a crime he didn't commit.
Through the years, there have been a lot of jailed
Black men who can identify with Joseph.

Once again, however, God enabled Joseph to tran-
scend his circumstances:

> The Lord was with [Joseph]; he showed him
> kindness and granted him favor in the eyes of
> the prison warden. So the warden put Joseph
> in charge of all those held in the prison.
> (Genesis 39:21-22)

Although Joseph again enjoyed favored
treatment, he was yet to experience his fourth type of
male wound, "collegial wounds" from close friends or
associates.

**Friends**

While he administered the prison, two men became the closest thing to friends that Joseph had. He
knew them well because he interacted with them often. One, a chief butler, and the other, a chief baker,
had both made Pharaoh angry. When they looked
sad, Joseph knew it was not like them and asked,
"Why are your faces so sad today?" (Genesis 40:7b).
They told Joseph about their dreams, which Joseph
interpreted for them, predicting restoration for one
man and execution for the other. It takes a dreamer
to help others make sense of their dreams. It takes a
visionary to help one understand a vision.

Joseph did not compromise because of friendship.
Proverbs 27:6 says, "Wounds from a friend can be
trusted." As sad as it was, the baker needed to know
the truth. Joseph told the butler the truth, too – about
his pending restoration and promotion. Joseph had
but one request, "But when all goes well with you, . . .
mention me to Pharaoh and get me out of this prison"

(Genesis 40:14). You would think that such a plea would ring in the ears of a friend forever. Just the opposite happened. "The chief cupbearer, however, did not remember Joseph . . ." (Genesis 40:23). Often men who become successful forget about the Josephs who helped them achieve their dreams. Nonetheless, in the planning of God, divine timing determines opportunity. Pharaoh, too, had a dream, ultimately jogging the butler's dormant memory, leading to Joseph's exercising his gift before the king. As a result, Joseph was promoted to the second highest office in the land.

God strategically used Joseph's man wounds to make him into a great leader. God used the familial man wounds of his brothers to get him out of the house and break his enmeshed ties with Jacob. God used the man wounds of the Midianites to get Joseph out of the pit. This, coupled with the communal man wounds of the Ishmaelites, got him out of their slavery into Potiphar's house. God used the vocational wounds of Potiphar to get Joseph away from the sexual temptation of the master's wife. God used the collegial man wounds to keep Joseph in prison until the proper time and occasion when he could fulfill his destiny. All the while, God was molding Joseph into a vessel suitable for a very important mission.

## Wounds and Scars

Joseph became the Nelson Mandela of his time, also going from prison to become leader of the nation which imprisoned him. Joseph, who had been labeled the villain by his brothers, would by divine orchestrating become the savior of those same brothers.

It was God who took Joseph from inmate to magistrate, from jailer to ruler, from prisoner to governor, from suspect to prospect, from being charged to being in charge, from law-breaker to law-maker. What enables a person to survive man wounds is the keeping power of God. Joseph experienced familial, communal, and vocational wounds – all at the hands of the men in his life.

Years passed, and Joseph – once a wounded man – became a scarred man. Often men say, "I'm not wounded anymore, but I still bear the scars." Scars are not bad. A scar is a mark left as a byproduct of the healing of injured tissue. Thus, scars are visible evidence of healing, monuments of recovery, and conspicuous testimonies of recuperation. Below are some differences between wounds and scars:

| Wounds | Scars |
| --- | --- |
| Open | Closed |
| Painful | Usually not painful |
| Release vital life | Retain vital life |
| Evidence of injury | Evidence of recovery |
| Often temporary | Often permanent |

Thus, God used both Joseph's wounds and his scars. His wounds made him a father to Pharaoh; his scars made him an agent of salvation to his family. His wounds made him a bringer of deliverance to his race; his scars made him the bringer of guidance to another race. His wounds helped him change the fate of his family; his scars helped him change the faith of the Pharaoh.

Even though our Lord is seated at the right hand of the Father with a new glorified body, the Father chose not to remove the scars. This is why Jesus was able to say to doubting Thomas, "Put your finger here; see my hands. Reach out your hand and put it into my side. Stop doubting and believe" (John 20:27). God can use our scars to turn faithless people into believers. He can use our emotional scars to show men that one can be severely wounded and recover to tell about it.

## Reconciliation

Joseph was eventually reconciled with his brothers. God used him to save the very men who had wounded him. He now understood the place of man wounds in his leadership development. He said to his brothers after revealing who he was:

Do not be angry with yourselves for selling me here, because it was to save lives that God sent me ahead of you . . . to preserve for you a remnant on earth and to save your lives by a great deliverance. So then, it was not you who sent me here, but God. (Genesis 45:5-8a)

## Conclusion

The punch line, the plumb line, the bottom line is this: our wounds – although inflicted upon us – are never just for us. Our wounds may also be the seeds of someone else's deliverance. The men who hurt us are the men we will often be used to bring deliverance to as leaders.

Jesus, our leader, was ultimately not wounded and scarred for Himself, but rather:

He was pierced for our transgressions, he was crushed for our iniquities; the punishment that brought us peace was upon him, and by his wounds we are healed. (Isaiah 53:5)

To be a Christian is to be a Christ imitator, to take up the cross, even as the Black man Simon of Cyrene did for our Lord. As we have seen from the life of Joseph, to become true leaders, we must concede that "man wounds" are not simply annoying, discomforting distractions, but rather a critical part of the process in making us into deliverance-bringing leaders.

# 13

---

# The African American Church Woman: Her Undeniable, Undebatable Leadership in Church and Society

by Mary Ross

*Mary Ross, Ph.D., is president of the Women's Department, National Baptist Convention, U.S.A., Inc. She serves on the boards of the Religious Alliance Against Pornography and Spelman College. A Chair of Excellence is being established in her honor at American Baptist Seminary. She is author and co-author of several books, including The* Minister's Wife *and* The National Missionary Study Guide. *Ross is editor of* The Mission.

Women are beginning to see today that Jesus did not display a demeaning view of women in word or deed. Moreover, He actually stood up to His contemporaries to defend women. The church in the centuries following, however, has largely conformed to cultural ideas about women.

## Historical Focus

Jesus acted naturally toward women, accepting them as full persons who could understand and respond intelligently to what He was saying. He discussed His mission with them and trusted women to go out and take the message to others (see John 4:7-42). Women were financial supporters of Jesus (see Luke 8:3). Several of the women who followed Him are better known to us through Scripture than are some of the apostles. Jesus was so different from the male disciples that on one occasion they "were surprised to find him talking with a woman" (John 4:27).

Both society and religion, whose images and symbolism are often intertwined, are experiencing a women's movement which is on the one hand exciting and at the same time frightening.

The movement is exhilarating because new possibilities are opening for both women and men. The change is frightening because a basic fear attaches to sexual identity, a fear of the unknown if comfortable traditional role expectations change.

Today, women are trying to extricate themselves from the three L's they have carried for centuries – labels, limitations, and low expectations. Traditionally religion has reserved the label of temptress for women. Further, the church has limited women to home functions; to serving children, the elderly, and the ill; and to subordinate positions in male-dominated organizations. The church has indicated its low expectations by discouraging women clergy, women seminarians, and women scholars.

In recent years, however, we are beginning to see women take more non-traditional leadership roles within the church.

## Foundation of the Church

Through the years from slavery to these significant nineties, the Black church woman has been the bedrock foundation in supporting the church of Jesus Christ, both with her sometimes meager earnings and with her highly gifted talent. She has shared, willingly, in support of the churches of her choice.

The African American church woman's faith and serenity make it possible for her to nobly accept that which cannot be changed and to change that which can be changed. Her faith and serenity enable her to meet disappointment and sorrow with inner poise. She knows, as Paul testified, that "in all things God works for the good of those who love him, who have been called according to his purpose" (Romans 8:28).

Through her many trials and tribulations, the Black church woman's spirit is ruled and regulated by the presence, peace, and providence of God. For certainly, in the language of the poet, her life "ain't been no crystal stair." Even today, she is still forced to grope in the dark. In spite of the obstacles, she continues to keep climbing.

According to a recent article in the *Spelman Messenger,* "Black women are filling the pews as church members at an estimated 70 to 80 percent, and they are no longer content to take [only] the secondary leadership roles designated to them throughout history: as missionaries, educators, fund raisers, and leaders of women's auxiliaries."

## Emerging Leadership Roles

The contemporary African American woman, with new career options open to her as a result of the civil rights and feminist movements, is still turning to "that old time religion," but with this exception: there is very little "old time" about it. Black women are entering divinity schools at an unprecedented rate. The *Los Angeles Times* reported recently that enrollment of Black women has increased over the last twenty years from less than one in ten to more than one in three African Americans in seminary!

This is good news and glad tidings. God grant that this African American church woman will continue to let the rule of God in her life be her priceless possession – the channel through which Jesus Christ may guide her decisions, inspire her will, and unveil unprecedented achievement in every phase of her living and giving.

In order to be a good leader, the Black woman must have a faith fit to live by, a self fit to live with, and work fit to live for. She knows, as Joyce Ladner says, "The Black woman's life has always been characterized by two major focuses: high achievement and excellence by a limited few, and a cycle of poverty that engulfs the lives of many."

In spite of the many problems that have been thrust upon her historically, she continues to fight for self-determination, equal opportunity, and a life that is void of discrimination based on sex, race, or social class. The social position of the Black woman is still fraught with the double jeopardy of being required to fight against both racial and sexual exploitation. Thus she continues to be a symbol of what it means to struggle to achieve under the most difficult conditions.

The Black church woman is aware of her position in the family and that the family is the most essential unit in the social structure, the basic unit of government itself. This goes to the very heart of our public institutions and democracy.

The only thing constant about the American family is change. Children in single-parent families are six times more likely to be poor and three times more likely to have emotional and behavioral problems than their peers from intact families. Nationally, more than 70 percent of all juveniles in state reform institutions come from fatherless homes. Teen suicide rates have doubled in the past twenty-five years. Every day 135,000 teens take guns to school.

There needs to be serious concern for troubled girls. They are growing up very fast. By age sixteen, some have slugged their way into gangs. By seventeen, many have their names stamped on police blotters. Girls are in trouble!

Based on precedents in various denominations, if something is to be done to curtail the troubles young people are having, it will be women who take the leadership. Yet the issues are so overwhelming that church women and church men should join hands and hearts in helping young people to solve their problems.

## The Black Family

In this time of rapid change in our society, it is imperative that the African American family and the church rescue the perishing in our community, which in turn must strengthen its institutions. The church must help the community to adjust to new circumstances and new challenges, increase financial support, and encourage more purposeful communication and collaboration.

The Black community is facing a crisis. The family and church can show leadership in how to help meet the challenge by keeping before the African American community the self-help tradition which is so imbedded in the African American heritage as to be virtually synonymous with it.

The family and church have the opportunity to show leadership by helping to make things happen, rather than just watching things happen or being among those who have no idea what happened. It has been said that few of us have a sense of urgency about what is happening to our society or about what is not happening in the church. As the family goes, so goes

the church. As the church goes, so goes the community. As the community goes, so goes our society, our
nation!

I challenge the African American church and
family to join hands and take the lead in their communities through voter registration drives, health
care programs, Children's Defense Fund activities,
crime patrols, Community Mobilization projects, par-
ent-teachers' meetings, and visiting their children's
schools without being summoned.

The Black family needs to be surrounded by encouragement, hope, insight, and strength. The *Wall
Street Journal* noted, "More than 100 million
Americans attend church every month, and about 30
million attend church four times a month, yet few of
our nation's professionals can be found in the pews
on any given Sunday." May the African American
church urge the community to take the lead in defin-
ing and addressing the new and continuing problems
it faces.

The Children's Defense Fund, in collaboration
with a wide range of denominations and religious organizations, sponsored a National Observance of
Children Sabbath in October 1994. Such an observance is worthy of support from the Black church, the
family, and the community.

Further, we cannot ignore childhood stress. One
in four school-age children experiences physical
illness because of stress-related factors. Children are
abusing drugs and alcohol at early ages. Again, I
challenge the African American church woman to
give of her best to help save our children!

Dr. Ethel Gordon quotes a very interesting selection from Ann Landers in *Help! The Family Is in
Deep Trouble*. Landers's "Advice to Parents from
Two Teen-age Children" recommends that parents
should avoid losing their temper, because children

imitate parents' behavior. Parents should not abuse booze or drugs. Children want and need to respect their parents. Parents should enforce strict, but fair, discipline. Young people need strong supports when they exhibit poor judgment.

Further, we must not forfeit the dignity of parenthood. Children need someone to look up to, someone who will be a model for them. Parents should not embarrass young people by trying to dress, dance, or talk like them.

Children want parents to show them how to believe in something bigger than themselves, such as God. In spite of what they say, children do not want parents to compromise on what is right. Nor do they want parents to be intimidated by children's threats to drop out of school or leave home.

In addition, children want parents who are always honest, who always tell the truth no matter what. Finally, effective parents are generous with praise. A few compliments will help children accept criticism more readily.

## The Relevant Church

Many communities are to be congratulated on having an ample number of African American church women ready, willing, and able to help their churches prepare to serve the needs of the soon-to-be twenty-first century. If the Black church is going to serve effectively, it must have the following relevant characteristics:

1. *A Teachable Spirit* – Successful congregations understand that there is always more to learn. They actively encourage members to develop new skills and to learn more about God and what He wants us to be and to do.

2. *A Bias Toward Indigenous Leadership Development* – For real African American leadership, look to grass roots. Leaders must be servants rather than celebrities. When I was a small girl, I often heard my grandmother sing a song which said, "I told Jesus I'd make Him a servant if He would write my name." That song at that time meant almost nothing to me; and I very much doubt if my grandmother grasped many of its deepest implications.

She did not know that to be a servant, every woman was her sister and every man her brother. She did not know that she owed a debt of concern for all and kindness to everybody everywhere. She did not know her duty to Christ obliterated all racial boundaries. She did not know that her responsibility to mankind transcended the geography of her immediate community, her country, and her nation.

One can see the appropriateness of leaders' re-examining their role as servants of the Eternal.

3. *Selflessness* – A relevant church has an upward, outward, and inward focus.

4. *Future Orientation* – Many churches focus on the past, but much remains to be done. It's not what they used to do, but what's happening now. Are they engaged in informing, performing, transforming, and reforming?

5. *Change* – A positive outlook toward change keeps the church on the cutting edge. The Women's Convention Auxiliary has adopted the following themes for the past two years respectively: (1) Charge, Change, Challenge; and (2) The Challenge to Choose Change Wisely in Church and Society.

6. *Cooperation* – Thrive on friendly cooperation among churches, councils, neighborhood workshops, and neighborhood watches.

7. *Mobilized Laity* – Volunteer workers should outnumber staff.

8. *Perseverance* – Keep on working. There is no time to coast along. This will entitle you to sing the Negro Spiritual, "I keep so busy serving my Master, I ain't got time to die."

9. *No Fear of Failure* – A church which is uncomfortable with failure will not be willing to take risks for maintaining effectiveness.

Many African American families are standing by able to help the church implement these characteristics to make a more relevant church. Unfortunately (but also fortunately!) some are waiting for the church to articulate a program that is sufficiently big enough to challenge them to get off the sidelines and into the game. Lest we forget, there are both responsibilities and new opportunities facing the African American church, which needs to become more aggressive in:

1. Empowering women to challenge oppressive structures, whether in the global community, their country, or their church.

2. Affirming – through shared leadership and decision making in theology and spirituality – the decisive contributions of women in church and community.

3. Giving visibility to women's perspectives and actions in the work and struggle for justice, peace, and the integrity of creation.

4. Enabling the churches to free themselves from racism, sexism, and classism – from teachings and practices that discriminate against women.

The church and family working together have an opportunity to promote a loving and just society, built upon biblical understandings of these concepts – a society that is humane in its treatment of all persons. The church and family have the privilege and responsibility of being the voice of the voiceless.

In essence, the African American Christian family is called upon to help the church remind society that all are a part of God's world – bound together as one family in the bundle of life – and that we must learn to live together. As a bright light shining in a dark world, we must demand justice for all of God's children, care for the sick, freedom for the enslaved, and so forth as we stand with our Lord in calling for a society of love, free of malice and greed.

# 14

---

# A New Breed

by Ja'Ola Walker

*Ja'Ola Walker, M. Ed., is vice president of Clarence Walker Ministries, Inc. She is active in counseling pastors and their wives.*

Our people are dying, sinking in despair, ignorance, violence, and fear. The destruction of our children and adults, like stench, is rising all around us. God is calling for a new breed of leaders, not just good men and women who are talented, intelligent, and brave. These are nice traits; but the destruction that is around us will require more than charisma, skill, and dedication. We need a supernatural anointing of God exploding in us and touching those around us.

It will take more than networking, positioning ourselves, and setting up ministries with good intentions. We need more than an occasional concern about drugs, poverty, and AIDS. This chapter explores these needs.

## A Divine Burden

First, we need men and women who have gotten a divine burden. They have found their own personal healing and set aside the weight and sins which so easily hindered them in the past. They have, instead, picked up God's burden for their people. The yoke of the Lord is easy and His burden is light, but it is still a burden. It is light because we don't have to carry it all alone. The new breed of leaders know they are taking orders from the Captain of the host, and they must do only what God is requiring them to do. Then they can enter into a rest of faith and trust Him for the outcome.

We don't have to be the sole saviors of our people or our world. To attempt such an unreasonable endeavor would only leave us burned out and more bitter. Jesus tells us:

> I tell you the truth, the Son can do nothing by himself; he can do only what he sees his Father doing. . . . For the very work that the Father has given me to finish, and which I am doing, testifies that the Father has sent me. (John 5:19, 36)

The new breed is to be contrasted with leaders who have no vision, burden, or concern besides themselves. The new breed is easily identified, not prone to seek the fat of the land, not manipulative, not controlling, and not greedy. Their ministry, business, or enterprise is not for the purpose of developing wealth, fame, and power for themselves. They do not disguise their motives with politically correct humanitarian and religious phrases, seeming noble to others and even to themselves. There is no room on their bottom line for the big "I." Helping their people is more than a byproduct.

They avoid the other class of leadership which moves to the opposite extreme. They have a burden and concern for their people, but do not try to become the savior of all that is around them, thereby avoiding ending up bitter and cynical as a result of the folks they are trying to help rewarding them by trying to destroy them.

As you exchange your burden for the Lord's burden, you will be inspired in a powerfully challenging way – but not beyond your resources and abilities, and not beyond your spiritual and physical strength. This is not to say that you will not be stretched. Your personal inspiration to help others may fade over the years. Folks may get on your nerves, hurt you, and abuse you. Your sense of brotherhood and racial camaraderie may soon sour. To avoid this, we as leaders need to cry out to God for His burden even as did the prophet:

Let the priests, who minister before the Lord,
weep between the temple porch and the altar.
Let them say, "Spare your people, O Lord.
Do not make your inheritance an object of
scorn, a byword among the nations.
Why should they say among the peoples,
'Where is their God?' "
Then the Lord will be jealous for his land
and take pity on his people. (Joel 2:17-18)

## Hearing from Heaven

Second, it is important for leaders to develop a hearing relationship with their heavenly Father. Before you seek mentors and leadership training programs, you must develop an intimate relationship with God so that you can hear from Him. Yes, God still speaks to His children in a variety of ways. No matter how He speaks to you, tune in. Hearing always requires paying attention, listening, being still, being quiet. We get so excited if Reverend Whoever or Bishop Somebody seems to take an interest in us. But promotion on all levels comes from the Lord. He puts down one and sets up another.

We too often forget the sovereignty of God. We spend our time "kissing up," compromising to fit in, and rubbing shoulders. We think the Kingdom of God is a large corporation run by the principles of Dianetics or Dale Carnegie's *How To Win Friends and Influence People.* While there are secular concepts which are useful in the Kingdom, we must get centered and know from whence our direction, motivation, and provision come. Otherwise, we will be used by others. They will open doors for us and close them at their pleasure. They will reward or punish us based on their human criteria. Some of our very brightest leaders have been bought and sold, not able to be true to themselves or to their God because someone else is footing the bill. Never giving God a chance to open doors, provide, or lead, they spend their time looking to people, leaning on the arm of flesh. They forget that He is the God who said:

Cursed is the one who trusts in man,
who depends on flesh for his strength
and whose heart turns away from the Lord.
(Jeremiah 17:5)

Historically, African Americans have been seduced into this position by persons from all walks: Jews, White America, our White Christian brothers, and even those of our own kind. Some leaders do not feel free to work at the deeper levels required for the deliverance of our people for fear of offending someone. We operate on a superficial humanitarian level that soothes the guilt of the majority culture, with a lasting ineffectiveness that is much like a Band-Aid being put on cancer.

Once you have accepted God's yoke and are able to receive direction from Him – once you have purposed in your heart that God, not man, is the Lord of your life – then is the time for you to set out on your journey to accomplish your divinely assigned destiny. Some leaders have actually gotten to this point but have failed to realize the need for continuous self-evaluation and other systems of accountability.

## Developing Accountability Systems

Third, we must continuously monitor ourselves for attitudes and thought patterns which lead to hidden personal sins which in turn lead to more obvious decadence and immorality. Leaders are on the top of Satan's hit list, and he is satisfied to begin with the small things we overlook – such as thoughts of jealousy, competitiveness, and strife – which must be identified and confessed. The more spiritually mature a leader is, the more subtle Satan has to be in his strategy to steal, kill, and destroy. Sometimes it seems as if our leaders are more insecure than other people. Some choose to be in leadership as a career option or to meet their emotional need for control, acceptance, or approval. Any outsider who is seen as a threat to the little kingdoms they have built will be dealt with accordingly.

Some aspects of African American culture make it difficult for many of us to work together and affirm others. This is clearly contrary to the biblical teaching regarding the unity of the body of Christ. As in so many other instances, Satan uses this weakness over and over to divide and conquer.

One problem that fuels this syndrome is a wrong measure of success – something remarkably akin to conspicuous consumption as noted long ago by E. Franklin Frazier in *The Black Bourgeoisie*. Leaders must not look at clothes, cars, buildings, and numbers of radio broadcasts as measures of success. Avoid the common question among preachers, "How many people have you got, Doc?" As if the number on the church roll were the one and only indicator of a successful life-changing ministry! There are some large churches filled with spiritually dead people. Although our fellow leaders may pat us on the back, God weighs us in the balance. He is our true evaluator, the One from whom we will get our report card.

As He did for the Laodicean Church, which represents our church age, Jesus is standing outside the door of some of these large "successful" churches saying, "Here I am! I stand at the door and knock. If anyone hears my voice and opens the door, I will come in and eat with him, and he with me" (Revelation 3:20). The unknown Jesus has been put out of many places, which continue to carry on their religious corporations, not seeming to notice His absence.

Other attitudes we must monitor include thoughts of lust, greed, and lasciviousness. Many in leadership begin to develop the notion that those they are leading are their private property. Without effective systems of accountability, power and fame begin to corrupt us, gradually causing us to cross forbidden boundaries. It is not enough to rationalize our behavior as "helping our people." Nor is it enough to surround ourselves with comrades who are in the same decadence. We dare not casually joke about who and how many of our women and men we have violated sexually. If we garrison our hearts with respect to smaller offenses, we will be stronger, better able to avoid the depths of depravity reported of some so-called leaders who have added wine, drugs, and sex to items of hospitality offered to visiting leaders.

Time and time again, history has recorded the rise and fall of our leaders. Even though their fall can be traced directly to a discernible pattern of deteriorating morality and integrity, rarely do we prepare our young men and women to deal with the moral pressures of leadership. This lack of training in such a foundational area is often related to the compromising lifestyles of those who teach the leaders-to-be. Sometimes the teachers have given in to temptation and immoral lifestyles themselves and don't feel comfortable addressing those issues in the lives of others. Because there is such a need for leadership in the African American community, we traditionally ignore the lifestyles of our leaders, satisfying ourselves with their charisma, strength, talent, and knowledge. However, we cannot be divine instruments of healing and deliverance for the people of God if we are using, violating, and raping them.

I don't know anyone who has gotten up and planned to destroy a successful ministry which he may have spent a lifetime cultivating. Major failures begin as small thoughts that trip us up on our journey. Thoughts that are not dealt with, confessed, and renounced will take root and destroy us in the end. This, of course, is the same process that Satan uses on all people. But because we are so visible as leaders, our fall will cause great tremors and repercussions in the spiritual world. If, for some reason, you do slip quietly into the next life without being caught, God will expose you to all of humanity, past and present, as our lives will be judged at the Judgment Seat of Christ. Yes, grace notwithstanding, we will be judged for the deeds done in the flesh.

> His work will be shown for what it is, because the Day will bring it to light. It will be revealed with fire, and the fire will test the quality of each man's work. If what he has built survives, he will receive his reward. If it is burned up, he will suffer loss; he himself will be saved, but only as one escaping through the flames. (1 Corinthians 3:13-15)

Keep short accounts. Deal with your own insecurities, fears, sins, areas of bondage, hang-ups, and complexes. Look past the applause, accolades, plaques, and write-ups in Christian magazines. Strive to allow the Lord to deal with your issues. Do not operate in pride and self-righteousness just because others tell you that you're successful. To God you are just His child who has a problem with fear, lust, or bitterness; and He wants to heal you.

God never waited until the heroes of the Bible were perfect to use them. Don't confuse the power of the blood and the Word with the perfectness of the vessel. God can use anybody. The gifts and talents you have come from Him. You did not win some contest to get these gifts. They are just that – gifts. God can use us while He is still in the process of working on us; so cooperate with that process. Get help from others when needed. You still need to be taught, counseled, comforted, advised, and encouraged to go on when you get tired.

You need godly people around you who love you and who will tell you the truth. The Bible says, "Confess your sins to each other and pray for each other so that you may be healed" (James 5:16a). Develop godly friends who can share with you and help keep you honest. You won't always feel free to confess to those under your ministry. Sometimes the Lord will lead you to share, but do so only as He leads.

Therefore, we need friends who love us without expectations. Some leaders have no friends because they are so busy competing and feeling threatened by everyone. Ask the Lord to lead you to Christians whom you can trust. Don't go by outward characteristics, but seek a oneness of spirit. The person may or may not have the same position as yours. Don't look down on people. Sometimes jewels are wrapped in seemingly insignificant packages.

Husbands and wives are to be an accountability system. Don't collude with your partner's craziness just to keep the peace. Speak the truth in love. "Honey, I love you, but I feel what you are doing is wrong." We often watch our mates backsliding and say nothing for a variety of reasons. That is not love. God doesn't want us to stay away from sin just to keep us from having fun. He knows sin is slowly killing us.

Make sure you get fed yourself regularly and systematically. Attend conferences and take in the Word. Avoid the temptation to criticize the speaker's hermeneutics, comparing yourself with him or her. Keep a teachable spirit. God can speak to you through even a child, but you must be humble enough to receive it.

That brings us to the thoughts of pride – the huge egos, the Nimrod complex that haunt our leaders: "I am the greatest." This attitude often creeps in when there is limited accountability and where the time spent in the presence of the Lord is at a minimum. It is easy to get caught up in the activity of leading. The pressures of crammed schedules, traveling, and achieving can cause us to completely forget our personal time with God. It is precisely during the time you stand quietly naked before the Most High God – having all your thoughts examined and revealed, your sins glaring like black spots in snow as you let God sweetly and firmly make adjustments, chasten, and sometimes scourge you – that you become aware of all the foul mess that is in you.

Oh, yes, staying in God's presence keeps you humble. He points out your jealousy, fear, gluttony, lust, and the like. He progressively deals with you concerning things other folks get away with, but which you can't get by with anymore. His goal is to transform you into the image of Christ even down to your thoughts, bringing them captive to the obedience of Christ.

When you stay in the presence of God, no one has to watch over you to make sure you behave. When women or men come with seduction in mind, the pull of temptation gets weaker and weaker. You will have victory not just physically, but even your thoughts will be pure as well.

## Guarding Family Relations

Finally, if the devilish plot to destroy you as a leader fails in all these areas, the enemy will try to attack your family. A number of leaders are wonderful men and women of God, but their ministries are hindered because of family problems. If you are not married, please realize that who you marry can either make or break you. It is a vital decision that should be made with the direction of the Lord. Don't put your life in compartments by thinking that your personal life and your ministry are separate. Every aspect of your life is a part of the process for fulfilling your divine destiny. Your marital partner is a major aspect of this.

On the other hand, if you are already married and realize you did not seek God for your marriage, realize that God can work even in a bad marriage for good for them who love God and are the called according to His purpose. Some of the most anointed folk have problems with their spouse and/or children; but they have learned to be obedient to God and pray through. In the midst of their suffering, God brings forth the peaceable fruit of righteousness.

There are no cut-and-dry formulas for addressing problem marriages. To begin with, you must get direction and have peace with God about your life. To address one specific situation which comes up frequently during my counseling sessions, I do not advise a woman to stay in the physical proximity if her safety is in danger.

If you are in a marriage where you believe you have the right person but you just have some challenges, then make marriage one of your priorities. Many leaders put their ministry before marriage and family, believing that somehow they are doing something noble and spiritual. We are to love the Lord first, address our own needs and those of our families next, and then minister to others. The Word says to love your neighbor as yourself. If you don't have a proper self-love, you will never be able to love and minister to your neighbor.

Of course, the Lord is the foundation. You can't do anything without Him. But if you are beat down mentally, physically, and spiritually, you will not be fit to meet anyone else's needs. Your spiritual health is important, as are your physical and mental health. No matter how anointed you are, if you abuse and neglect your body, you will suffer the consequences. God says your body is His temple and if you abuse it He will destroy it. You can't fulfill your destiny if you are in heaven ahead of time because of abusing your body.

Husbands and wives are one. They are part of each other. How can you meet the needs of all those around you and neglect the physical, emotional, or financial needs of your mate or those who come from you (your children)? A biblical criterion for leadership is one's ability to rule his own house. *Rule* does not just mean lord over. A good ruler loves, provides, nourishes, and protects his house. Ministry to others follows. Build your family relationship by getting teaching, counseling, and obeying God's principles of marriage. Make time for family.

There is nothing more fulfilling than finding God's destiny for your life and flowing in it. As the power of God flows through the uniqueness of who you are, lives will be touched in a special way. You won't have to try to preach like so and so, whoop like this one, or sing like that one. The main thing will be what God can accomplish through your uniqueness. Husbands and wives must find a purpose bigger than having a house in suburbia, fighting about petty things, chairing some committee, or getting some position. When you have discovered your divine purpose as a couple, it will bring solidarity, unity, intimacy, and fulfillment.

## African American Princes

Many of our leaders have gotten caught up doing many wonderful things but missing God's assignment. Once you have deciphered your assignment, you must establish priorities and focus your work. This will cut down on jealousy, competition, and one part of the body slandering another part. You won't have time to worry about what other folks are doing. It will take all your time and energy to find and fulfill your place in the body of Christ. Each member of the body is important. Leaders cannot complete the work without the help of others.

This represents the new breed that God is calling for today. It is more than wishful thinking on my part. It is the fulfillment of a biblical prophecy concerning our people in the last days.

Princes shall come out of Egypt; Ethiopia shall soon stretch out her hands unto God. (Psalm 68:31, KJV)

These princes are the cream of our people. They will not necessarily be who we would choose. We clamor for leaders who look like King Saul – those who are tall, handsome, and striking. Like the ancient Israelites, we value the wrong things. God is raising up Davids who may seem insignificant. When Samuel came to anoint the new leader, David's own father did not even bother to call him in from his chores to be in the lineup.

God is putting a war cry, a burden, in leaders' innermost being as they look at the condition of people all over the world. They have the desire to want to lead with integrity which many times makes them look odd among some of our current leaders. They sometimes even bring out feelings of rage and fear in others because the King Sauls can see God's hand on these princes' lives.

This new breed has various and sundry callings, gifts, and ministries which are often unique and unusual; including poetry, art, dance, preaching, teaching, drama, business, and music. In their hearts, they know it will take more than traditional church to reach this last-days, sex-crazed, drug-addicted, violence-prone, crazy generation. They know it will take more than standing in the doors of the church, playing "Just As I Am," and beckoning to the passing crowds to come.

The new breed feels the urge to go into the highways and byways, leaving the security of the church knowing that our light is needed in the midst of the darkness of the world. They are tired of church politics, denominationalism, division, strife, and folks having a form of godliness, but denying its power. They are tired of watching the devil get bolder and bolder about stealing minds and influencing people with his psychic networks, new age movies, demonic toys, and subtle witchcraft taking over our media. They are tired of seeing people on television developing spiritual powers of darkness as they yield more and more to Satan, while we church people sit around talking about what God can't do anymore, not yielding to God and not letting Him touch our daily life, our emotions, our will, or our decisions.

God wants to explode His power in us, through us, and around us. But first, we as leaders must come out of our bondages, our Egypts. We will be used of God to lead Ethiopia (our people) to soon stretch forth her hands to God in praise.

Many major church leaders today – including Billy Graham – have said that there is a great revival coming in the last days and that Black people will be the key. Who better to bring real reconciliation between the races in the body of Christ than those who have been stepped on the most! After all, we are partners with Jesus in the ushering in of an upside-down Kingdom. As we let God heal and empower us, we will see Him positioning us to impact the world. He will open doors and develop this network and many resources in unusual ways. No one person, group, movement, board, or organization will be able to structure this or take the credit. It will be done by God, without our permission, without our committees.

As God winds up time and we prepare for the last day events, we are scheduled to go out in triumphant glory as a church. God will be doing a lot of moving, shaking, putting up one, putting down another, and pouring out His Spirit on all flesh. Old men will dream dreams. Young men will prophesy. Even lowly servants and handmaidens will be poured out on by the Holy Spirit. God is stepping out of our traditions, our unbiblical rules, and our hang-ups. He is going to show the world and His church that He is a consuming fire.

Learn to work together. There are no spiritual Rambos, as my husband says. We wrestle against the forces of darkness as a team. If you begin your ministry focusing on your specialty area where God has equipped and anointed you, don't feel as if you have to branch out into other areas of ministry just because someone else is doing it. You don't have to reinvent the wheel. Make use of others' resources, materials, and expertise. Do your part; and know that as we network, support, encourage, pray for, and finance each other – together as a body – the job will be accomplished. Don't spend forty years in the ministry and miss God.

Another syndrome that leads to the moral decay of our leaders is the "good boy, good girl" syndrome. This is the false belief that because of our positions, if we just try hard enough we will be able to please God and make Him proud. It took years for God to get this through my head – that it is not my righteousness. All of my righteousness is like dirty stinky rags to God.

There is no good thing in our flesh. Your sin nature will deceive you and make you think you can live holy on the strength of your own moral fiber, dedication, and good intentions. But as you continue in His presence, the light of His holiness will expose sin in you that shocks even you. Our motives, attitudes, agenda, corruption, and decay – covered with the glitter of tinsel and plastic – often looks shiny and impressive to the world and to ourselves. But God sees through it.

We may even have the nerve to get self-righteous about ourselves, comparing ourselves to ourselves, forgetting that it is only God's goodness, mercy, and grace that enable us to be effective. God must supernaturally love others through us. His fruits of righteousness must be developed in us. Our sin nature must be crucified daily. We must "reckon," or consider by faith, our sin nature to be crucified with Christ along with our rebellion and fears, bad temper, lust, bitterness, anxiety, unbelief, gossip, and strife. Don't assume that because you are Rev. So-and-So you don't have to go through this basic routine daily. Let God rule your life and empower you to live right.

The standard for living right is not your denomination, not what your bishop laid down, not your church's bylaws. It is, rather, the standard set for us in the Word. Some of us try to be super spiritual. We set up restrictions for folk that go above and beyond the Word of God, feeling that we can use rules and man-imposed restrictions to "make" folk live right. We do well to be concerned for folk who adhere to many rules in the light but in the dark break every one of them. However, we cannot legislate righteousness. Our standard is the Bible, and it will take the power of the Holy Spirit to change people. Rather than trying to legislate holiness, fill the hearts of the people with the Word. Focus on helping them to develop a good, intimate, vital relationship with God. It is the Holy Spirit's job to "lead us into righteousness," to convict, and to convince us of sin. If we fill our churches with the praises of God and honor His presence, He will touch people's hearts.

We must also avoid going to the other extreme, modeling to our people that sin is not a big deal because God will forgive us. Leaders from this school of thought impose fewer rules and are more obvious about their sin. But God's rules do not change; and the consequence for breaking them is still death – the death of our ministries, relationships, finances, health, children, community, business, peace, safety, and sanity. Obviously, as you look at our people, we are a dying race, and we live in the midst of dying races. We have rebelled and disregarded God's laws long enough. The generation after us is already in bondage to drugs, violence, and ignorance. If we do not turn to God, we will not continue to serve them.

## The Conclusion of the Matter

Based on my years of ministry, I have presented four principles which are essential for godly leaders: getting a divine burden, developing a hearing relationship with God, monitoring self thus developing accountability systems, and strengthening the family. I have no illusion that these are new revelations.

These are things we all know in our heads. But as my husband and I counsel and speak, traveling all around the country, God has opened doors in every denomination. We see homes, marriages, lives, and ministries of men and women of God crumbling all around us. These are not men and women who don't know God's Word. They are well equipped, educated, and talented. But the attack of Satan is fierce, and these leaders are falling in great numbers.

God's solution is always simple and I encourage you – no, I beg you – to turn your heart to God for the sake of our race and for the sake of other races to whom we may be called to minister. Be sober and vigilant because your adversary is trying to destroy you. He wants you to leave your wife or husband, have an affair, sleep around, abuse your family, and destroy your children by being one way at home and another way to the world. He wants to pull you into pornography, drugs, alcohol, depression, bitterness – whatever he can – to make you ineffective. But God also has an agenda. Believe me, it will be done with or without you or me. No one is indispensable to God. He will find men and women. He will let you die wandering in the wilderness and, if necessary, use those from the prisons and streets – saving, healing, and making them new.

God will have a voice in the last day. He may even step over our organized religion and take His program to the streets. But His agenda will be completed. With or without you and me, the body of Christ is going to go out of this age in a blaze of glory.

# 15

---

# Some Leaders Are Born Women

by Lorraine Elizabeth Williams

*Lorraine Elizabeth Williams, Litt.D., is producer and on-air personality of "Let's Talk," a weekly Christian television talk show seen on national cable systems. An ordained minister, national speaker, and long-time community activist, Williams is also a consultant to the Pittsburgh Leadership Foundation.*

Leadership, like character, is somewhat difficult to describe but easy to recognize when you see it. In *Leadership Jazz,* Max dePree characterizes leadership as "finding one's voice and connecting it to one's touch.... A leader voices the expression of one's personal set of values and beliefs; a leader's touch demonstrates competence and resolve."

Leadership is generic, neither male nor female. Leaders are accountable. They are servants. Leaders have integrity in all things. Leadership is constructive. Leaders stress quality in addition to or instead of quantity. They trust the spoken word, intuition, and their "gut." Effective leaders value teamwork and cooperation.

A leader is people-oriented and capable of listening. A leader is honest, emphasizing motivating people. A good leader promotes affirming group relations while motivating the team to get the job done. Social transformation occurs when visionary leadership is in place. Great Christian leaders bring liberation, dignity, reconciliation, and a sense of destiny and purpose to the complex issues that often govern society. Visionary leadership is instilled by long-term planning. Visionary leadership is established by a firm understanding of self and is matured by strong conviction, by taking risks, and by learning from mistakes.

**Role Models**

There are a number of women who have impacted my life positively. Some of them are:

1. My fifth-grade teacher, Jean Hixon, a private pilot.

2. My piano teacher, Mary Richburg.

3. My first Sunday school teacher, Mrs. Carrie Simon, who captivated me weekly and whose class I refused to leave.

4. Rev. Brown, assistant pastor of Wesley Temple A.M.E. Zion Church in Akron, Ohio, who gave me my first glimpse into what the power of God means, not only in preaching but also in living.

5. Of course, there's my mother, Marguerite Nash, who – encouraged by my dad, James R. Nash – began an effective one-person crusade to rid the neighborhood of taverns. With that success, she maintained the momentum, established the West Akron Citizens Council that eventually led to political activism, was elected vice-president of the NAACP, and became the matron of the Summit County jail where she brought her own kind of networking and compassion to nurse women back to wholeness in her unique way.

## Seeing Opposition as a Challenge

I am grateful for the successes God has granted me over the years. But I must say that my experience has not been without opposition. The prophetic and pastoral nature of leadership is often misstated to be gender specific. It takes an Abraham-like faith to persevere in spite of the roadblocks and obstacles leaders have to overcome. We need to learn to make allies of those who have difficulty seeing beyond their own struggle for significance and who may be intimidated by the obvious respect, strengths, vision, unique talents, and skills cultivated through persistence, training, education, and maturity which may make one qualified for a job.

## The Need for Coalitions

History informs us that, as descendants of African people, we need partnership and collective effort to restore dignity to our communities. Together as male and female we are a vibrant and radiant expression of the Creator. Our gifts, working together, can promote wholeness, healing, and reconciliation for the entire community. Culturally, leadership by Black women is not unique. We are the descendants of great African queens such as Ann Nzinga, Candace, Cleopatra, Nefertite, Makeda, and Sheba – women who ruled vast empires and made their nations great.

Western culture and philosophy have taught women to support leaders and exercise power through others. In addition, the prevailing American culture has made it imperative for the African American woman to assume a strong leadership role. Had she not risen to the challenge, our communities would be in a sad state indeed. One challenge we face as a people is how to empower both our males and females to a position of shared leadership in order to advance our people at a faster rate.

As we approach the twenty-first century, it is necessary for marginalized groups to form coalitions that are committed to the development of healthy communities and the implementation of culturally inclusive practices. Lack of information and services is a barrier for progress in the urban community. One result is that low-income families are not sufficiently empowered to access the services available to them. Visionary leadership will bring the technical training to these pockets of poverty to enable them to function as fully participating members of society. Indigenous leadership must come from the bottom for it to affect the entire community.

Black women, spiritually awakened and visionary, have become social architects and have moved into the mainstream of community activism. Poverty, racism, and increasing crime rates have driven women to network, build support groups, and develop strong tenant societies and block organizations. In addition, women have sought political office in order to be advocates for marginalized people.

Israel, suffering under an oppressive slave system in Egypt, managed to multiply its seed. In a similar vein, the 1990 census reported 14.6 million African American males and 15.4 million females in this country. In the midst of this present age, Black mothers, too, are producing a generation of young people who have the potential to become future national leaders.

## Essentials for Women in Leadership

In order for women to develop in their role as leaders, there are several things that must occur:

*1. Identify those who can help you in your growth and development.*

Take a low profile as you work to attract relationships that will ultimately enable you to network into powerful insider groups. Judge others in terms of their track records on items which affect your constituents.

**2. Build a research portfolio to capture information and current trends for potential leaders.**

Building new models of ministry involves mentoring, teaching, training, and negotiating models that can be easily applied in the smallest to the largest context.

**3. Develop and identify female leadership styles.**

Analyze and recognize different personality types and leadership styles. This helps a leader determine administrative and organizational styles she will feel most comfortable with and discover which are best suited for maximum success. Strong leaders avoid divisive competition while encouraging productivity-stimulating creative competition among groups.

**4. Emphasize results through positive experiences so that women plan and structure their involvement.**

Develop a database and resource clearinghouse of reproducible models of ministries. This will help clarify the power base, guide the development of strategies, and facilitate the delicate process of negotiation in order to sharpen the focus and direction of the organization.

**5. Relate compassionately and cross-culturally with other women.**

Leadership needs to continue to broaden personal and professional networks with a wide variety of individuals who are willing to invest their physical and material resources. This is accomplished as you (1) encourage dialogue between diverse groups on pertinent social and spiritual issues; and (2) serve as a catalyst for cooperative events.

6. **Expose women to appropriate examples of empowerment.**

Communicate verbally and in writing openly and regularly. Do not assume that others are informed. Develop a forum in which needs can be addressed. Cultivate and maintain working relationships with advisory boards and funding entities in local, regional, and national foundations and corporations.

7. **Promote, train, and establish mentoring relationships with women.**

Spend time getting to know your field staff and key persons. Stay on top of turf issues and hidden agendas. Encourage constituency to be up front about their needs.

8. **Establish and define standards of excellence. Identify training needs through surveys and other research.**

Master your field. Be the best. Quickly identify problems and move on.

9. **Develop a permanent, self-sustaining network.**

Maintain relationships with governmental and special services agencies, universities, public and parochial schools, churches and parent organizations as well as with civic and fraternal associations which have concerns related to your interests.

A comprehensive study of women in urban ministry needs to be undertaken. The scale of women's involvement in ministry and the magnitude of their contribution are remarkable. Yet, written histories have largely overlooked women. These women serve as role models for women who juggle busy schedules in today's world – women who may not be able to minister full time, but who may be able to lead where the needs are greater.

# 16

---

# Mentoring Tomorrow's Leaders

*Barbara Walton of Atlanta, Georgia, is a highly sought-after conference speaker. She feels that a stranger is a friend she has never met. Barbara has mentored a large number of leaders over the years.*

There is one thing that I learned from gardening: You can't have a harvest if you never plant a seed. Even after you plant the seed, God gives the increase. So it is clear that I can't take credit for my little contribution to developing the leaders of today. The Lord sent young men and women to me over the years. We talked. And now they are leaders.

## Mentoring, Bible Style

A mentor is an experienced and trusted friend and adviser. The most natural mentors are one's parents and grandparents. Excellent examples are Lois and Eunice, as Paul acknowledges to Timothy, "I have been reminded of your sincere faith, which first lived in your grandmother Lois and in your mother Eunice. . ." (2 Timothy 1:5).

I often reflect on 2 Kings 2 for its interesting side-light on the mentor and the students. Although Elijah trained numerous prophets (2 Kings 2:3, 5, 7), it was Elisha whose commitment led him to follow his mentor to the very end. Twice Elisha asked other student prophets not to dwell on the sadness they all felt about Elijah's impending departure to heaven. Three times he begged Elijah not to deny him the opportunity to serve the aged mentor up to the moment of his departure to heaven. As a result, Elisha's reward greatly exceeded that of the other student prophets. He received Elijah's mantle of leadership as well as a "double portion" of Elijah's spirit. This proved to be excellent equipping as Elisha endeavored to discharge the will of God for his life.

Elisha and other biblical role models became models for my life. I cannot say that I ever regretted the time and effort that went into each of my mentoring contacts. In fact, if the truth be told, I feel that I always received as much as I invested in those young people. Most of the time, I didn't even think of myself as being a mentor. I was just being me.

If there is anything that I majored on doing, it was to support the young person in his or her own decision-making. Some of their decisions were better than others, but they needed the opportunity to think through their decisions with a supportive, but objective, person – one who would be there for them to help them evaluate the results of a poor decision.

Above all, I did not want to be like the man who tried to help a butterfly to get out of a cocoon while avoiding the natural struggle that goes along with this process. The result was that the winged creature emerged, but was too weak to survive in this cold, cruel world. My advice to all leaders and would-be mentors is not to stifle developing young people in your commendable desire to help them to grow. Give them lots of room to try their wings. Remember, we learn from failures as well as from successes. But stay around to help them pick up the pieces.

Hopefully, there will be more celebrations than failures.

## Kitchen Talk

My job at Carver Bible Institute was one of the most important. No, I wasn't a professor or administrator. I was the cook. My job was to keep a variety of healthy food on the dining room tables for the students and staff. Many days after a meal (sometimes before) one or more of the young people would stop in the kitchen just to talk. And the Lord knows I love to talk. Sometimes the conversation would be friendly and relational. At other times it would gravitate toward some weighty matter on the student's mind. I would do a lot of listening before I would speak. I asked a lot of questions about how the student was understanding the issue, what the options were, and which option would bring the most glory to God. We prayed a lot. Usually they answered their own questions.

Occasionally, the student would not know how to process the issue and I would suggest a way to begin. Occasionally, I would offer not one, but several, good options for consideration. It was not my place to make a person's decision for him or her. Several of my student friends decided to enter the leadership ranks as pastor, missionary, or ministry leader. Here are a few selected examples:

## Matthew Parker

I remember a quiet young man from the Black Bottom of Detroit, the first in his family to attend college. As I recall, he had had few solid Christian role models before he came to Carver. The professors made themselves available to Matthew as they did to all the students. However, it seemed that Matthew preferred to visit me in the kitchen and at my home. (He loved to eat.) We talked and talked and talked during his time at Carver. In fact, we stay in touch even now, almost two decades later. I valued the desire for service that I sensed in Matthew. I valued him as a child of God. He began to discuss his classes with me. I still remember how he would beam when he showed me his grades each semester.

I later learned that Matthew considered me his spiritual mother. He told me how much he appreciated that our dialogue about his concerns always proceeded from a scriptural base. Today, Matthew is president of the Institute for Black Family Development. He is a consultant and a preacher. He still enjoys telling me about his travels, like when he met President Reagan, Billy Graham, Chuck Colson, Pope John Paul II, James Dobson, John Perkins, Tom Skinner, Dolphus Weary, Tony Evans, and others. Matthew counts on me to remind him not to place his confidence in knowing people who have achieved worldly or even spiritual success.

I must admit that I have been impressed with the way that God selected Matthew to become principal of a Christian school, organizer of the National Summit of Black Christian Leaders, assistant vice-president of William Tyndale College, convener of the National Conference on the Family, and so much more. Most of all, I am pleased that he is now a devoted husband to his lovely wife Karon and a good father to their four children.

## Clifford Ice

Another young man who used to spend a lot of time in my kitchen is Clifford Ice. As I recall, Pastor Ice was a bright young man who appreciated having someone older and wiser to speak with about the many exciting things that he was learning and contemplating. He displayed considerable wisdom, maturity, and godliness as we explored various options.

He made a valuable contribution to the Bible study that met in my home.

As the Bible study grew into a church, Clifford was called to be the pastor. I am so glad he decided to enter the pastoral ministry and that he is now my pastor at Community Bible Chapel here in Atlanta.

## Malletor Cross

One young lady I really enjoyed fellowshipping with is Malletor Cross, who is co-superintendent of Detroit Afro-American Mission, Inc. Ever since I met her, she has been so full of vim, vigor, and vitality, with a burning desire to read her Bible and to pray. We had such rich dialogue. She often asked my opinion on matters such as Christian service, godly living, and other spiritual and practical issues. We talked like sisters. She has provided me with valuable insights as well. I value her friendship even to this day.

Malletor has become quite a teacher, Christian leader, and conference speaker. Her attitude has been right. She has subordinated her own desires to those of the Master. She and her wonderful husband have raised six beautiful children to the glory of the Lord while serving Him.

## Availability

To hear some people talk, it seems as if mentoring would be extremely complicated. I have found that sharing naturally is the essence of being a mentor. All Christians have a measure of faith. We all can testify of how God has provided triumph over our trials. We all can testify to the times when we have been obedient to God when it would have been easier and seemingly more profitable to be disobedient. All of us have homes, food, and wisdom which can be shared. Tell young people what helped mold your relationship with God and how He taught you to love your spouse, your children, your friends, and – of course – your enemies.

It is important to be supportive when a young person makes a decision in the Lord, whether or not it seems to be the best decision possible under the circumstances. Of course, we should share our wisdom; but we dare not fail to assure the person that we will stand by him or her no matter what. Decision-making can be taught. It can be caught. However, the ability grows only when a person is allowed to make decisions and to see the results of those decisions.

It is not necessary for me to give a long, complicated formula. The main thing is to be a friend, to ask questions, to share from your heart, and to be available. A lot of the time, people will be discouraged or simply uninspired to strive for greatness. This is nothing that a lot of encouraging and exalting the name of Jesus can't cure.

It seems that just about everywhere I travel, I run into some of the young people who used to visit my kitchens. I had no idea that God would use me as a mentor to so many on their way to significant service for Him. I only responded to the students' expression of interest. Somehow the Lord superintended our conversations so that we always talked about the things that were most important to the young people. I was available; but so were they. We had such rich times of prayer and Bible study. Today, even though my students – my friends – are all over the globe, they still stay in touch.

I learned from those experiences that it is not so much your ability that God looks for – as your availability.

# 17

## Called to Lead an Existing Organization

by Eugene Seals

*Eugene Seals, M.B.A., president of Quality Publishing Systems, is co-author of* The Wild Thing. *He taught urban ministry at William Tyndale College and now teaches business, computers, and communications at Wayne County Community College. An agent for authors, Seals has edited a number of books, including* What's Up With Malcolm?, Have You Got Good Religion?, *and* Waite: A Man Who Could Not Wait.

For various reasons in the life cycle of a ministry, the incumbent president may move on to a higher calling. After a careful search, the board of directors issues a call to you to come to their Macedonia and help them. How will you handle the new assignment? Many new presidents seem to follow the old adage, "A new broom sweeps clean." As soon as they assume leadership of the organization, they release the "lieutenants" who may possibly still be loyal to the previous administration. There are a lot of hard feelings with this approach. The organization generally would not be what it has become without some very dedicated effort on the part of the "lieutenants," to say nothing of the contribution made by the entire staff.

Leadership in the African American church and ministry needs to proceed from a clear Christian basis. Whereas management consists of such tasks as planning, organizing, staffing, budgeting, controlling, and climate setting, Christian management should also consider that the Bible teaches that only two things are eternal: God's Word and people. The purpose of this chapter is to illustrate how this consideration affects one's approach to leading people.

## A Good Secretary

Very soon after I became executive director of the venerable Detroit Rescue Mission Ministries, a board member asked if I would like to replace the existing secretary, since she may have some loyalty to the previous president. I felt that her prior experience would be a valuable asset to my office. As time went on, she proved to be an invaluable resource, rescuing me more times than I can count. It would have been much more difficult if I had brought in a new person who would have had to learn her job at the same time I was busy learning my own.

Selecting, training, and retaining a faithful, competent secretary is one of the most important staffing decisions a manager must make. The process could take lots of time. The benefit is that a good secretary can make you two or three times more effective than you would be otherwise. A manager can always replace a person later if he or she does not work out in a given job. But I saw no need to replace an individual simply for fear that there may be a question of loyalty.

## A New Organization

Instead of spending the time to recruit and train a new secretary, I was able to address myself to understanding the board, the staff, the clients, the contributors, the funding sources, our mission statement, and how we were organized to accomplish that mission. As I reviewed these interrelated elements, I noted that we had grown to a $3 million operation but had an organization more suited to a much smaller scope and a previous mission statement.

My second major task, then, became developing, in conjunction with the board of directors, a new organization that would address itself more directly to the current mission and scope of the ministry. The new structure included a couple of new positions. For example, our operations had grown to four divisions, with ten buildings in multiple locations of the city plus a ranch in the country. Our maintenance budget was sizable. So I created a director of maintenance position, promoting a young supervisor and giving him a new vision of his ability to contribute to the ministry. He rose to the occasion.

We were able to fill all the new positions from within except one which called for a different level of credentials than we had on staff.

## Christ-Centered Ministry

Endeavor to keep Christ first in all your business and busy-ness. When working with my new staff, I led a devotional at the beginning of each weekly management meeting and the monthly all-staff meeting. This provided an opportunity for me to show my reliance on the Word of God and to show how Scripture applied to our ministry. Often space was allowed for comments regarding the subject of the devotional. The process of preparing the devotionals increased my own understanding of the primacy of Christ in what we were doing. As the agenda unfolded, we often wrestled with how our deliberations and our decisions measured up with the scriptural mandate.

After demonstrating the general concept of using the Scriptures, a meditation, and prayer at each meeting, I rotated that responsibility among the members of the management team and encouraged them to work at having devotions in their staff meetings.

## Upgraded Reporting

There were enough computers in the organization for each director to begin to produce top quality reports for my use and for the monthly board meetings. One director began experimenting with developing statistics on the vital measurements of success in his division. These reports were valuable in assessing the cost-effectiveness of our programs. One funding agency in turn used our reports in setting standards for administration of other programs they funded throughout the state.

A manager does not have to plan everything. For example, we had a devoted former client who had been added to the staff and who lived in one of the residential apartments. With careful money management, he put most of his earnings in the bank – until he discovered computers. When I met him, he had purchased his fourth computer which he used on his job and during the extra hours which he loved to volunteer. To my dismay, I discovered that if that man would be called away for an extended period of time, his division's billing operation would suffer. So, although it was not necessary for me to plan the introduction of computers into the billing operation, I felt a need to take steps to train an additional person in case he would be away when bills had to be issued.

## Maximizing Potential

Even while we were sharecroppers, my parents stressed the value of education. My dad excelled through grade three and my mother was outstanding and would have gone on to greater academic achievements than the eighth grade had she been born in a different decade or in a state other than

Mississippi. Thanks to my parents, I encouraged education for everyone in our organization.

With the management team settling into its new structure, I noted that the rest of the staff also required upgrading. Instead of replacing them, I hired a trainer who had business degrees, work experience at General Motors, and experience as a school teacher. His assignment was to develop, under my direction, a curriculum to train my staff to be more professional in their approach to the day-to-day business of being a Christian-based human services agency.

This consultant shared with me recently that my encouragement led to his becoming a sought-after trainer and subsequently a principal of a private school. He has turned down offers to take more lucrative jobs. He tells me I helped him find his niche. From my point of view, I was simply using the principle of leverage: upgrading my staff, while helping his career. That is a principle that comes pretty naturally to me.

We didn't limit ourselves to in-house training. I sent people to relevant seminars on company time, at company expense, including reasonable costs for meals. We sent key staff persons to state and national meetings of their professional associations in order for them to stay on the cutting edge of developments in their area.

We encouraged staff to pursue additional education, preferably related to our mission. Because of my contacts, I was able to arrange for one employee to be awarded a tuition scholarship to pursue a master's degree. It was easier for me to ask for the money from a private donor since it was not for me.

## VIPs: Staff and Clients

Having learned from Dale Carnegie the importance of acknowledging the value of people, I set up luncheons twice a week with a carload of staff persons representing each division. These were times of getting acquainted with persons who did not report directly to me and not to pursue a formal agenda. We talked about the individuals, their families, their careers, and their feelings about their work. We talked about me, the weather, and so forth. There is a certain social distance that many leaders maintain from people who do not report directly to them. I find that an excessive distance is a barrier to an effective organization. More importantly, the Bible tells me that the ground is level at the foot of the cross. It was a little awkward at first for the staff to accept that they did not have to call me Mr. Seals, that I was genuinely interested in them as persons, that my "door was always open." I am happy to say that no one abused the open door policy. They seemed to feel good just knowing I was accessible, that our conversations would be treated in confidence, that I would recommend how they should approach difficult situations sensitively. It was a blessing to see individuals grow through that process.

There seem to be too many meetings in both business and ministry. Always ask, "Is this meeting necessary?" The monthly all-staff meeting was designed to keep employees informed about the direction of the ministry and about administrative changes that might affect them. Correct information eliminates the possibility for error. The all-staff meetings were excellent times for recognizing personal, family, or job-related achievements.

One person thanked me for calling those meetings, and told me that previously she had had no idea what was going on in one of the other divisions. So, I noted that a valuable byproduct of the meetings was an increase in team spirit, a sense of identification with the entire scope of the ministry.

As with any organization, there was too much work for the leader to do it all. Through the revised organization structure, I delegated authority and responsibility to my directors, trusting the managers and their people to be responsible for doing the work of the ministry. I concentrated on interfacing with the managers, the board of directors, donors, and funding sources.

I had no time to worry about whether some person might take my job. I had not grasped for the job in the first place. The Lord had led me to the assignment through a young man whom I had met at William Tyndale College. Besides, the ministry grew fast enough that each person's job was expanding about as rapidly as his or her ability to grow. The growth could not have been accommodated so smoothly if my team had been kept on a short leash. Of course, I did meet with the team as a group and individually on a weekly basis. When necessary, I met with a given director more regularly. In addition, I discussed my directors regularly with the board's personnel committee.

Never having managed such a large staff before, I was frankly surprised to find out how many people needed to be disciplined and even released. It occurred to me that our mission should not be limited to rehabilitating the street people, addicts, prisoners, and abused women and children in our care. The same concern needed to be extended to those on our staff who were giving their lives to help restore our clients to become productive members of society. And so we did, in the process rescuing many who might have received harsher treatment somewhere else. One such person is now a supervisor in the ministry. One difference between a secular organization and one run on Christian principles is the extent to which we work at reconciliation and restoration.

In retrospect, I question my decision not to allow a promotional internal transfer where a person would have been supervised by his brother-in-law. I should have relied more on my evaluation of their ability to work together successfully. Instead, we will never know if that might have been a good move for the individual and for the organization. However, I believe it is important to hear your trusted advisers and supervisors. And they strongly recommended against it.

My philosophy was that clients were not persons who were put there to inconvenience us. Rather, they were our very reason for existing. We were a *therapeutic community* (one where staff encouraged clients to share responsibility for their own recovery). We knew that the best therapy comes from the Lord and from His Word. We could see a vast difference in the clients who embraced Jesus. Those who did not accept Jesus had a more difficult recovery. In fact, a larger percentage of them returned to their evil ways after they graduated from our programs, if in fact they stayed to graduate.

Since Jesus came a long way from heaven to bail me out of a predicament worse than death, I felt that I should journey to our several facilities in order to rub shoulders with our clients. Now that was an interesting experience for me! All I knew about illicit drugs came from the movies. So the guys were able to tell me a thing or two. Little did I realize the impact that those visits would have on the clients years after they graduated from our program. Often when I run across an alumnus, he or she expresses appreciation that I did not consider myself too important to converse with clients or eat with them. It seems to have been a great boost to their self-esteem.

Let me hasten to add an important point. Keep all relationships with clients – as well as with staff, with the board, and with others – above board. Proceed with due caution. Our headquarters and main ministries were located in the Cass Corridor, a.k.a. the Skid Row of Detroit. You wouldn't confuse that area with a Sunday school picnic. It looked a lot like bombed-out downtown Beirut. A number of the street people looked like war refugees. In all the nights when I was the last person leaving the building – as uncomfortable as I might have felt – no one ever bothered me. (It was reported, however, that some years earlier a director's wife had given a ride to a client who in turn assaulted her in broad daylight.)

Still, keep in mind that the world system is designed to exact every ounce of retribution, and more, from an offender or from anyone who is down. The last thing they need is for a Christian rehabilitation agency to operate from the same flawed philosophical-theological base.

## Dealing with the Opposite Sex

When a man makes a mistake, he can sleep it off, work it off, or relocate and start over. This is also true of women to some extent, unless their situation involves dependent children. It is an indictment on our society that so many men – whether Black, White, Asian, Christian, non-Christian, or what have you – can walk away from their responsibility to dependent children. For years, it has been the maternal instinct that has been the salvation of children. And even that is breaking down more and more.

We had a number of women and children in a small, but growing, division of the ministry, which was operated by female staff. I spent a fair amount of time with those staff persons and pursued their professional development the same as I did for the men and women who worked in the other ministries. They always insisted that I join them for a meal when I would visit their division. Talking over food or over a cup of tea helps bring understanding. I began to learn what I had taught to aspiring missionaries using a tongue-in-cheek expression, "When we parachute you into Pogo-Pogo, the first thing you should do is drink a lot of tea." That is – get to know the people you will be ministering to.

People don't care how much you know until they know how much you care. The staff was capable of administering the program; they had done quite well prior to my arrival. I simply wanted them to understand something of the heart of the new leader who was making the decisions that would enable them to discharge their ministries with dispatch. In addition, meeting the clients gave me a greater appreciation for the relevance of the decisions that I had to make and the proposals that I had to formulate for meeting the needs of the men, women, and children who came to us when they had nowhere else to go.

My philosophy was not to do any heavy duty managing at their location, and not to find myself alone with any of the females, whether staff or client. Private meetings with female staff were conducted only in my office with its glass door and no curtain.

## Respect

A president has respect conferred on him by virtue of his appointment by the board of directors. The public ceremony and the press releases are nice for the scrapbook. But they go only so far with the people who want to know legitimately, "What have you done for me lately?" It is easier for staff and clients to respect a leader whom they know, even if only slightly. They are smart enough to know that you have important work to do and that you can't spend your entire work week with them. The fact that you reach out to get to know them and to let them know you helps to earn respect and understanding. They know that not every decision will go their way. And they can accept that from one whom they know is a person of integrity and who has their best interest at heart.

The opposite is likewise true. There is often suspicion surrounding decisions made by a leader who is distant, who is preoccupied with what he thinks are more important matters than the staff and clients he is called to serve.

## Management by Walking Around

Owners of businesses do a lot of things naturally which are later taught in business school. One such concept is Management by Walking Around, a term popularized by John Naisbitt in his best-selling book *Megatrends.* No smart owner sits in his or her ivory tower while the hired help run a multi-million dollar operation. I recall how Ross Perot made headlines by even going into GM dealerships to observe how the dealers were promoting the products. For my own part, I made it a practice to get out of my office as often as possible. Management can make better policies when we know more about what is happening on the front lines.

## Personnel Replacement

It is important to discern whether a new task can be done with existing personnel or whether additional staff is required. Whenever possible, I lean toward creating ad hoc (temporary) teams for projects which have a limited time span. A good case study of this occurred in connection with the free public health clinic which we operated. Many of our neighbors preferred our clinic above the city hospitals and clinics which were contracted to provide medical services to them. The medical treatment was the same. What was different was that the medical director created the kind of atmosphere where our volunteer professionals treated the patients with utmost respect. I enjoyed visiting the clinic because the staff was always in a good mood.

One professional met the Lord while volunteering at the clinic. Over the years, she and her daughter became the backbone of the clinic and an asset to the overall ministry.

I noted that the clinic operated out of a meager 300 square feet of dedicated space. On clinic night, volunteers used a portion of the dining area as a waiting room and commandeered three counselors' offices (themselves carved out of the dining room). There had been talk for a long time about converting the Tabernacle, a large underused building, into a clinic, boardroom, and multi-purpose facility. My feeling is that talk isn't worth the paper it is printed on. With my bias for action, I appointed a task force to study, plan, and implement the project.

When weekly reports indicated no progress, I met with the leader of the ad hoc committee. We agreed that his strong suit was not construction project management. Another manager was given the assignment, and the project moved ahead at a rapid clip. Upon the facility's completion, the community loved it. Because of the enormous increase in space, we were able to expand services. It is important to take assertive action to work with people from their position of strength. In order to do this, there must be continuing dialogue with the staff to ensure that they and the leader understand their strengths, and limitations. A leader is successful only if his people are successful.

## Fiscal Accountability

Our income was derived from a combination of donations, grants, and government reimbursement for services provided. We treated all revenue as a sacred trust. In walking around, I observed instances where we could improve in our stewardship of funds.

Seldom was the situation urgent, so I would address such observations in my private meetings with the responsible manager. In addition to the sacred trust dimension, I noted that any improvements we could make would provide funds to help me upgrade salaries. This appeal to enlightened self-interest was effective with some people.

There were two instances, however, where I found myself angry with a manager for not being aware of what was happening to one of his buildings and to one of his food storage areas. Neglect can very quickly lead to having to spend more money later in order to rectify what had been a small problem originally.

When it comes to money, I operated with a hands-on approach. Managers were allowed to spend budgeted funds. However, periodically I would ask them to explain why they chose a particular course of action. I performed regular reviews of our financial situation, including signing most of the checks. We had a hard-working chief financial officer with unimpeachable integrity who was responsible for the monitoring in that area. Still I insisted on being kept informed. The buck stopped at my desk. Too many organizations go out of business because of the way the money is handled. In addition, my reputation was on the line.

## The Bottom Line

Ministry differs from business in the following very important respect: Business has no ambivalence about its objective. A contemporary saying is, "No matter what they tell you the subject is, they are talking about money." I have been amused by the variety of platitudes found in mission statements where I have been employed:

To serve the community. . . .

To produce the best products. . . .

To be the technology leader in our field. . . .

Not on your life. These are not mission statements. They are strategies. Even secular human services agencies know the difference between mission and strategy. A friend's boss told him as recently as 1994, "Do whatever it takes to keep those at-risk kids in school (mission) even if you have to lead them to the Lord (strategy)."

Our mission was to restore people (clients) to their families, their churches, and their communities. My vision was that the term "people" in our mission statement should be interpreted in the broadest sense, certainly to include also the staff who devoted themselves to accomplishing the mission for the clients.

My commitment to take care of the staff was tested in an unexpected manner. I received a call from one of our divisions. The police were there with a warrant to arrest a valued counselor. It seems that the long arm of the law had stretched over a 600-mile expanse and a number of years and found him – except he was no longer the same. Onesimus, we will call him, was thoroughly reformed. He explained that in his former life, he had left his hometown in a hurry with money that belonged to his employer. He had lived it up in places like Las Vegas before coming to the end of his rope in Detroit, where our folks had been instrumental in working with him through a painful detoxification process, helping him to an alcohol-free life, and leading him to the One who is able to do exceedingly abundantly above all that Onesimus had ever thought possible.

He saw displayed vividly that God forgives, but that often we still have to suffer the consequences of our misdeeds. I assigned my most tenacious employee, "Eliezer," to follow up on Onesimus. I wrote letters to the local authorities, to Onesimus's hometown authorities, to his court-appointed attorney. I offered to be responsible for him – but not for his debts! Onesimus agreed that we could withhold a large amount from his paycheck to pay the old debt. I kept my board informed of my plans and interest in my employee and brother. They approved my initiatives.

I sent Eliezer to Hometown for Onesimus's court hearing. The details are fuzzy to me now, but went something like this. On the hearing date, a deputy unlocked Onesimus's cell and told him that he did not need to go to a hearing, that he was free to go with Eliezer. The deputy remarked that Onesimus "must know somebody big." Onesimus replied that he didn't know anybody, but *Somebody* knew *him*. He was surprised to see Eliezer waiting for him. Eliezer, in turn, was surprised that Onesimus was being released. The next day Eliezer showed up at my office, remarking that he had a surprise for me – at which he produced Onesimus. I found out how Rhoda must have felt in Acts when Peter appeared at the door. *What are* you *doing here?* I thought, in joyful amazement that he was back, grinning from ear to ear.

Onesimus expressed his gratitude for my intervention in his case. I assured him that it was no more than right. Onesimus had helped hundreds of men find their way back to a productive life, one of whom I know is pastoring a church right now. Helping Onesimus seemed to be the least we could do. A nice serendipity was that word got around that I was concerned about my people. Talk about a morale boost that money can't buy!

As the months came and went, Onesimus began to complain about the bite that the wage garnishment was having on his paycheck. I reminded him that he could be doing time with no paycheck at all. He agreed and praised the Lord.

And that's what we have to do. Both leaders and staff people need to be reminded, in the immortal words of Wadean Parker, "We are all ex-offenders."

# 18

A Text for Our Times

We have shared from our hearts what we believe to be effective approaches to the critical issues which face ministries today. It is no mistake that this book emphasizes the positive. Our authors see their task as that of helping a sister or brother along the way.

Our motivation for writing is to spur you on to excellence. A popular bumper sticker says, "God made me; and God don't make no junk." Excellence involves more than technique. For further research you are encouraged to attend training seminars sponsored by The Urban Alternative, the Christian Management Association, the American Management Association, the Charles E. Fuller Institute, various Christian colleges, and any number of other traveling workshops. Most are reasonably priced, especially in comparison to the enormous benefits. In addition, you should consider becoming a working member of a national association composed of other leaders in the same ministry or professional area as yours.

Another invaluable technique is to spend a day with a ministry leader on location or to engage a number of leaders in individual conversations at the various conventions. People love to share what they are doing. Not only can such a field trip produce ideas for solving nagging problems, but you will often develop new vision for your ministry as well.

Many of the ideas in this book are the result of years of study, experience, tears, and prayer. You can shortcut much of the time and the agony of trial and error by benefiting from the wisdom presented by our writers. Much of leadership is caught as contrasted to being taught. Few leaders can get around the concepts addressed in this book. The ones who do are those who are fortunate enough to be able to delegate them to an executive vice-president. Even then, that person has to address the thorny issues. They will not go away.

Periodic review of this volume will assist both existing and emerging leaders as you formulate approaches to address everyday problems confronting your ministry.